Jumanji Feast: 96 Culinary Marvels Inspired by the Film

Bahamian Conch Fritters Hut

Copyright © 2023 Bahamian Conch Fritters Hut
All rights reserved.
:

Contents

- INTRODUCTION 8
- 1. Jungle Curry 10
- 2. Safari Skewers 11
- 3. Vine-wrapped Grilled Fish 13
- 4. Jumanji Jackfruit Salad 14
- 5. Wild Boar Tacos 16
- 6. Monkey Bread 17
- 7. Elephant Ear Pastries 19
- 8. Python Pesto Pasta 21
- 9. Zebra Striped Cupcakes 22
- 10. Crocodile Kebabs 24
- 11. Waterfall Smoothie Bowl 26
- 12. Quicksand Quinoa Bowl 27
- 13. Rhino Ravioli 29
- 14. Baboon Banana Bread 31
- 15. Mangrove Sushi Rolls 33
- 16. Lion's Mane Mushroom Risotto 34
- 17. Tarzan Tiramisu 36
- 18. Ostrich Omelette 38
- 19. Rockslide Rockfish 40
- 20. Gecko Gingerbread Cookies 41
- 21. Jaguar Jambalaya 43
- 22. Coconut Cannonballs 45
- 23. Python Pizza 47
- 24. Snakefruit Salad 48
- 25. Water Buffalo Wings 50
- 26. Bazaar Banana Split 51
- 27. Monkey Magic Muffins 53

28. Panther Pumpkin Soup 55
29. Jungle Juice 56
30. Elephant Eclair 58
31. Tiger Tail Twizzlers 60
32. Safari Sundae 61
33. Quicksand Quiche 63
34. Vulture Vinaigrette Salad 65
35. Python Pie 66
36. Viper Vermicelli 68
37. Leopard Lemon Bars 70
38. Wild Boar Burger 72
39. Tarantula Tacos 74
40. Hyena Hash 75
41. Rhino Ramen 77
42. Jumanji Jerky 78
43. Crocodile Ceviche 80
44. Bamboo Shoot Smoothie 82
45. Python Popcorn 83
46. Cobra Crepes 85
47. Monkey Mango Sorbet 86
48. Leopard Latte 88
49. Jungle Jello 89
50. Watermelon Waterfall 91
51. Baboon Banana Smoothie 93
52. Elephant Eye Eggs 94
53. Ostrich Oreo Cake 95
54. Rockslide Rock Candy 97
55. Vineyard Viper Veggies 99
56. Lion's Mane Lemonade 100

57. Tarzan Tart 102

58. Zebra Ziti 104

59. Quicksand Quinoa Salad 105

60. Water Buffalo Biscuits 107

61. Mangrove Margarita 109

62. Rhino Root Beer Float 110

63. Panther Pecan Pie 112

64. Python Pumpkin Pancakes 113

65. Baboon BBQ Ribs 115

66. Elephant Endive Wraps 116

67. Monkey Mango Salsa 118

68. Leopard Lollipop 119

69. Cobra Coconut Curry 121

70. Crocodile Crème Brûlée 123

71. Tiger Tail Tarts 125

72. Jungle Jam 127

73. Quicksand Quail Eggs 128

74. Vulture Vegetable Stir-fry 130

75. Python Pita Pockets 131

76. Hyena Honey Glazed Ham 133

77. Water Buffalo Blueberry Muffins 135

78. Rhino Raspberry Ripple Ice Cream 136

79. Leopard Lime Lollipops 138

80. Baboon Basil Pesto 140

81. Elephant Ear Éclairs 141

82. Monkey Mocha Latte 143

83. Cobra Coconut Cupcakes 145

84. Quicksand Quiche Lorraine 146

85. Tarzan Tofu Tacos 148

86. Viper Veggie Volcano 150
87. Leopard Lemon Lava Cake 151
88. Water Buffalo Blue Cheese Burger 153
89. Rhino Rainbow Rolls 154
90. Python Peanut Butter Pie 156
91. Baboon Black Bean Brownies 158
92. Elephant Eye Edamame 159
93. Monkey Maple Syrup 161
94. Jungle Jicama Salad 163
95. Cobra Cornbread 164
96. Vulture Vanilla Vinaigrette 166
CONCLUSION 168

INTRODUCTION

Step into the wild and embark on a culinary adventure like never before with "Jumanji Feast: 96 Culinary Marvels Inspired by the Film." This extraordinary cookbook invites you to explore the fantastical world of Jumanji through the lens of gastronomy, where the magic of the screen seamlessly fuses with the allure of the kitchen. With 96 tantalizing recipes inspired by the beloved Jumanji film franchise, this cookbook is a feast for both the eyes and the taste buds, promising a culinary journey that transcends the boundaries of imagination.

The Jumanji films, known for their captivating blend of adventure, humor, and a touch of the mystical, have left an indelible mark on audiences around the world. In "Jumanji Feast," we pay homage to this iconic cinematic universe by transforming its enchanting landscapes and characters into delectable dishes that bring the magic of Jumanji to life on your dinner table.

Our culinary journey begins with a nod to the lush jungles and mysterious creatures that populate the Jumanji world. From Sticky Spider Rolls that pay homage to the arachnid challenges faced by our heroes, to Lizard King Skewers inspired by the reptilian wonders of Jumanji, each recipe captures the essence of the film's rich tapestry and infuses it into your dining experience.

Venture further into the heart of Jumanji with a selection of mouthwatering mains that draw inspiration from the thrilling quests and challenges faced by the characters. Savor the bold flavors of Forbidden Fruit Salad, a vibrant medley of exotic fruits inspired by the forbidden realms of the game. Indulge in Smoldering Brisket Tacos, a fiery tribute to the charismatic character played by Dwayne "The Rock" Johnson, whose culinary counterpart is as bold and unforgettable as the man himself.

As we navigate through the diverse landscapes of Jumanji, we encounter desserts that are nothing short of magical. Dive into the delectable world of Monkeying Around Banana Bread, a playful dessert that captures the mischievous spirit of the jungle's inhabitants. Delight in the savory sweetness of Jewel of Jumanji Cheesecake, an homage to the precious gemstones that play a pivotal role in the films.

"Jumanji Feast" is more than just a cookbook; it's an immersive experience that allows you to recreate the enchantment of Jumanji in your own kitchen. Each recipe is crafted with precision and creativity, ensuring that your culinary creations not only taste exquisite but also transport you to the heart of the Jumanji adventure.

Whether you're a seasoned chef or a kitchen novice, "Jumanji Feast" invites you to step into the magical realm of Jumanji, where the ordinary becomes extraordinary, and the flavors are as bold as the challenges faced by its intrepid characters. So, buckle up, gather your ingredients, and prepare to embark on a culinary journey that transcends the boundaries of reality – because in the world of "Jumanji Feast," every bite is an adventure waiting to unfold.

1. Jungle Curry

Transport yourself into the heart of the mysterious Jumanji jungle with this flavorful and adventurous Jungle Curry. Inspired by the wild and untamed spirit of the film, this curry is a tantalizing blend of exotic spices and vibrant ingredients that will take your taste buds on a thrilling journey.

Serving: 4 servings
Preparation Time: 15 minutes
Ready Time: 40 minutes

Ingredients:
- 1 lb boneless, skinless chicken thighs, cut into bite-sized pieces
- 2 tablespoons vegetable oil
- 1 large onion, thinly sliced
- 3 cloves garlic, minced
- 1 tablespoon ginger, grated
- 1 red bell pepper, sliced
- 1 green bell pepper, sliced
- 1 cup bamboo shoots, sliced
- 1 cup baby corn, halved
- 2 tablespoons green curry paste
- 1 tablespoon red curry paste
- 1 can (14 oz) coconut milk
- 1 cup chicken broth
- 2 tablespoons fish sauce
- 1 tablespoon soy sauce
- 1 tablespoon brown sugar
- 1 teaspoon ground turmeric
- 1 teaspoon ground cumin
- Salt and pepper to taste
- Fresh cilantro leaves for garnish
- Cooked jasmine rice for serving

Instructions:
1. In a large pot or wok, heat the vegetable oil over medium heat. Add the sliced onions and sauté until they become translucent.

2. Add the minced garlic and grated ginger to the pot, stirring continuously for about 1 minute until fragrant.
3. Add the chicken pieces to the pot and cook until they are browned on all sides.
4. Stir in the green and red curry paste, coating the chicken evenly.
5. Pour in the coconut milk and chicken broth, and then add the fish sauce, soy sauce, brown sugar, turmeric, and cumin. Mix well.
6. Add the sliced red and green bell peppers, bamboo shoots, and baby corn to the pot. Season with salt and pepper to taste.
7. Bring the curry to a simmer, then reduce the heat to low, cover, and let it simmer for 25-30 minutes, allowing the flavors to meld and the chicken to cook through.
8. Serve the Jungle Curry over jasmine rice, garnished with fresh cilantro leaves.

Nutrition Information:
(Per Serving)
- Calories: 450
- Protein: 25g
- Fat: 28g
- Carbohydrates: 20g
- Fiber: 4g
- Sugar: 6g
- Sodium: 1100mg

Embark on a culinary adventure with this Jumanji-inspired Jungle Curry, and let the bold flavors transport you to the heart of the jungle!

2. Safari Skewers

Embark on a culinary adventure with these delightful Safari Skewers inspired by the thrilling film Jumanji. Transport your taste buds to the heart of the jungle with a medley of flavors that capture the essence of the wild. These skewers are not only a treat for the senses but also a nod to the unpredictable and exciting journey that awaits in the world of Jumanji.

Serving: Makes 4 servings
Preparation Time: 15 minutes

Ready Time: 30 minutes

Ingredients:
- 1 pound boneless, skinless chicken breasts, cut into bite-sized pieces
- 1 cup pineapple chunks
- 1 red bell pepper, cut into chunks
- 1 green bell pepper, cut into chunks
- 1 red onion, cut into chunks
- 8-10 cherry tomatoes
- Wooden skewers, soaked in water for 30 minutes

Instructions:
1. Preparation:
- Soak wooden skewers in water for at least 30 minutes to prevent them from burning during grilling.
- Cut the chicken into bite-sized pieces and prepare the pineapple, bell peppers, red onion, and cherry tomatoes by cutting them into chunks.
2. Assembling Skewers:
- Preheat the grill or grill pan to medium-high heat.
- Thread the marinated chicken, pineapple, bell peppers, red onion, and cherry tomatoes onto the soaked skewers, alternating the ingredients for a vibrant and flavorful mix.
3. Grilling:
- Place the skewers on the preheated grill and cook for about 10-15 minutes, turning occasionally, until the chicken is cooked through and the vegetables are slightly charred.
4. Serve:
- Remove the skewers from the grill and let them rest for a few minutes.
- Serve the Safari Skewers on a platter, and enjoy the adventurous flavors inspired by Jumanji.

Nutrition Information:
(Per serving)
- Calories: 280
- Protein: 28g
- Carbohydrates: 25g
- Fat: 8g
- Fiber: 5g
- Sugar: 15g
- Sodium: 60mg

These Safari Skewers are a perfect addition to your Jumanji-themed feast, bringing a taste of the wild to your table. Enjoy the flavors and savor the memories of the jungle as you indulge in this delicious and adventurous dish.

3. Vine-wrapped Grilled Fish

Transport your taste buds to the adventurous world of Jumanji with this delectable recipe inspired by the lush jungle scenes of the film. Vine-wrapped Grilled Fish combines the essence of the wild with a tantalizing burst of flavors. This dish captures the spirit of the untamed, offering a culinary journey that mirrors the unpredictability of the Jumanji game itself.

Serving: Serves 4
Preparation Time: 20 minutes
Ready Time: 40 minutes

Ingredients:
- 4 white fish fillets (such as snapper or cod)
- 1 cup fresh cilantro leaves
- 1 cup fresh parsley leaves
- 3 cloves garlic, minced
- Zest and juice of 1 lemon
- 1/4 cup olive oil
- Salt and pepper, to taste
- Banana leaves or grapevine leaves (for wrapping)
- Lemon wedges, for serving

Instructions:
1. Prepare the Marinade:
In a blender, combine cilantro, parsley, minced garlic, lemon zest, lemon juice, olive oil, salt, and pepper. Blend until you achieve a smooth, vibrant green marinade.
2. Marinate the Fish:
Place the fish fillets in a shallow dish and pour the marinade over them. Ensure each fillet is well-coated. Allow the fish to marinate for at least 15 minutes, allowing the flavors to infuse.

3. Preheat the Grill:
Preheat your grill to medium-high heat. If using banana leaves, briefly heat them on the grill to make them pliable.

4. Wrap the Fish:
Lay out banana leaves or grapevine leaves. Place a marinated fish fillet on each leaf, then wrap the fish securely, creating individual parcels.

5. Grill the Fish Parcels:
Grill the wrapped fish parcels for about 10-15 minutes, turning them halfway through. Cooking time may vary based on the thickness of the fillets. The fish is ready when it easily flakes with a fork.

6. Serve:
Unwrap the grilled fish parcels and transfer the fish to serving plates. Garnish with additional fresh herbs if desired and serve with lemon wedges.

Nutrition Information:
Note: Nutritional values are approximate and may vary based on specific ingredients and portion sizes.
- Calories: 300 per serving
- Protein: 30g
- Fat: 15g
- Carbohydrates: 5g
- Fiber: 2g
- Sugar: 1g
- Sodium: 400mg

Enjoy the flavors of Jumanji with this Vine-wrapped Grilled Fish—a dish that combines the thrill of the jungle with a symphony of tastes that will transport you straight into the heart of the adventure.

4. Jumanji Jackfruit Salad

Step into the enchanting world of Jumanji with this delightful Jackfruit Salad, inspired by the magical film that takes you on a wild adventure. Bursting with tropical flavors and vibrant colors, this salad is a celebration of the lush and exotic landscapes found in the Jumanji universe. The starring ingredient, jackfruit, brings a unique and hearty texture, making this salad a satisfying and nutritious dish for any occasion.

Serving: 4 servings
Preparation Time: 15 minutes
Ready Time: 20 minutes

Ingredients:
- 2 cans (20 oz each) young jackfruit, drained and shredded
- 1 cup pineapple chunks, fresh or canned
- 1 cup cherry tomatoes, halved
- 1 cucumber, diced
- 1 red bell pepper, diced
- 1/2 red onion, finely chopped
- 1/4 cup fresh cilantro, chopped
- 1/4 cup fresh mint, chopped
- 1/2 cup feta cheese, crumbled (optional)
- 1/4 cup roasted cashews, chopped

Instructions:
1. Prepare the Jackfruit:
- Rinse and drain the canned jackfruit. Shred the jackfruit using a fork or your hands, mimicking the texture of pulled pork.
2. Assemble the Salad:
- In a large mixing bowl, combine the shredded jackfruit, pineapple chunks, cherry tomatoes, diced cucumber, diced red bell pepper, finely chopped red onion, cilantro, and mint.
3. Optional: Add Feta Cheese:
- If desired, add crumbled feta cheese to the salad for a creamy and tangy element.
4. Toss and Garnish:
- Gently toss the salad ingredients until well combined. Top the salad with roasted cashews for a delightful crunch.
5. Serve:
- Divide the Jumanji Jackfruit Salad among serving plates. This salad can be enjoyed on its own or as a refreshing side dish.

Nutrition Information:
(Per Serving)
- Calories: 280
- Total Fat: 10g
- Saturated Fat: 4g

- Cholesterol: 20mg
- Sodium: 380mg
- Total Carbohydrates: 40g
- Dietary Fiber: 6g
- Sugars: 20g
- Protein: 8g

Embark on a culinary adventure with this Jumanji-inspired Jackfruit Salad, a delicious nod to the fantastical world of the film. Whether you're a fan of the movie or simply looking for a flavorful and nutritious salad, this recipe is sure to transport your taste buds to the heart of the jungle.

5. Wild Boar Tacos

Embark on a culinary adventure inspired by the wild and untamed world of Jumanji with these delicious Wild Boar Tacos. As you savor the flavors of this exotic dish, imagine yourself traversing the dense jungles and encountering the unexpected, just like the characters in the film. The rich and robust taste of wild boar paired with vibrant toppings will transport you to the heart of the game.

Serving: 4 servings
Preparation Time: 20 minutes
Ready Time: 2 hours (marination time included)

Ingredients:
- 1 pound wild boar meat, cubed
- 1/4 cup olive oil
- 2 cloves garlic, minced
- 1 teaspoon cumin powder
- 1 teaspoon smoked paprika
- 1 teaspoon chili powder
- Salt and pepper to taste
- 8 small flour tortillas
- 1 cup shredded red cabbage
- 1 cup diced pineapple
- 1/2 cup crumbled queso fresco
- 1/4 cup chopped fresh cilantro
- Lime wedges for serving

Instructions:
1. In a bowl, combine olive oil, minced garlic, cumin powder, smoked paprika, chili powder, salt, and pepper to create the marinade.
2. Place the cubed wild boar meat in a resealable plastic bag and pour the marinade over it. Seal the bag and massage the marinade into the meat, ensuring it's evenly coated. Marinate in the refrigerator for at least 1-2 hours, allowing the flavors to meld.
3. Preheat your grill or grill pan over medium-high heat.
4. Thread the marinated wild boar cubes onto skewers, or use a grill basket, and grill for about 8-10 minutes, turning occasionally, until the meat is cooked through and has a nice char.
5. Warm the flour tortillas on the grill for about 30 seconds on each side.
6. Assemble the tacos by placing a generous portion of grilled wild boar on each tortilla. Top with shredded red cabbage, diced pineapple, crumbled queso fresco, and chopped cilantro.
7. Serve the Wild Boar Tacos with lime wedges on the side for a burst of citrusy flavor.

Nutrition Information:
(Per serving)
- Calories: 450
- Protein: 24g
- Fat: 18g
- Carbohydrates: 48g
- Fiber: 5g
- Sugar: 8g
- Sodium: 620mg

Indulge in these Wild Boar Tacos and let your taste buds journey through the wild landscapes inspired by the magic of Jumanji.

6. Monkey Bread

Embark on a culinary adventure inspired by the magical world of Jumanji with our delightful Monkey Bread recipe. This sweet and gooey treat mirrors the unpredictability and excitement of the Jumanji game itself. As you savor each bite of this pull-apart masterpiece, let the flavors transport you to a realm where the line between reality and fantasy blurs.

Serving: 8-10 servings
Preparation Time: 15 minutes
Ready Time: 2 hours (including rising time)

Ingredients:
- 3 1/4 cups all-purpose flour
- 1/4 cup granulated sugar
- 1 package (2 1/4 teaspoons) active dry yeast
- 1/2 teaspoon salt
- 1/2 cup unsalted butter, melted
- 1/2 cup milk, warmed
- 1/4 cup water, warmed
- 1 teaspoon vanilla extract

For Coating:
- 1 cup granulated sugar
- 1 tablespoon ground cinnamon
- 1/2 cup unsalted butter, melted

Instructions:
1. Prepare the Dough:
- In a large mixing bowl, combine 2 cups of flour, sugar, yeast, and salt.
- In a separate bowl, whisk together melted butter, warm milk, warm water, and vanilla extract.
- Add the wet ingredients to the dry ingredients and mix until well combined.
- Gradually add the remaining flour until a soft dough forms.
- Knead the dough on a floured surface for about 5-7 minutes until it becomes smooth and elastic.
2. First Rise:
- Place the dough in a greased bowl, cover it with a damp cloth, and let it rise in a warm place for 1 hour or until doubled in size.
3. Assembly:
- In a small bowl, mix sugar and cinnamon for the coating.
- Grease a Bundt pan with butter.
- Pinch small pieces of dough and roll them into balls.
- Dip each ball into melted butter, then coat in the sugar-cinnamon mixture.
- Layer the coated dough balls in the prepared Bundt pan.
4. Second Rise:

- Cover the pan with a damp cloth and let the dough rise for an additional 30 minutes.

5. Baking:
- Preheat the oven to 350°F (175°C).
- Bake the monkey bread for 25-30 minutes or until golden brown.
- Allow it to cool in the pan for 10 minutes.

6. Inverting and Serving:
- Invert the monkey bread onto a serving platter.
- Serve warm, allowing everyone to pull apart the sweet, gooey pieces.

Nutrition Information (per serving):
- Calories: 380
- Total Fat: 18g
- Saturated Fat: 11g
- Cholesterol: 45mg
- Sodium: 150mg
- Total Carbohydrates: 50g
- Dietary Fiber: 2g
- Sugars: 20g
- Protein: 5g

Indulge in this Jumanji-inspired Monkey Bread, and let the cinematic magic come alive on your taste buds!

7. Elephant Ear Pastries

Step into the magical world of Jumanji with these delightful Elephant Ear Pastries. Inspired by the lush and mysterious jungle setting of the film, these sweet treats are a perfect blend of crispy, flaky layers and a cinnamon-sugar coating that will transport your taste buds on an adventure of their own. Whether you're a fan of the classic Jumanji or the modern adaptations, these pastries are sure to be a hit at any gathering.

Serving: Makes approximately 12 elephant ear pastries.
Preparation Time: 20 minutes
Ready Time: 40 minutes

Ingredients:

- 1 sheet of puff pastry, thawed
- 1/2 cup unsalted butter, melted
- 1 cup granulated sugar
- 2 tablespoons ground cinnamon
- Powdered sugar for dusting (optional)

Instructions:
1. Preheat the Oven:
Preheat your oven to 375°F (190°C) and line a baking sheet with parchment paper.
2. Prepare the Elephant Ears:
a. Roll out the thawed puff pastry on a lightly floured surface.
b. Brush the melted butter evenly over the entire surface of the puff pastry.
3. Create the Cinnamon-Sugar Mixture:
In a bowl, mix together the granulated sugar and ground cinnamon.
4. Coat the Pastry:
Sprinkle the cinnamon-sugar mixture generously over the buttered puff pastry, ensuring an even coating.
5. Fold and Cut:
a. Fold the pastry in half lengthwise, pressing gently to seal.
b. Cut the folded pastry into 1/2-inch strips.
6. Twist and Bake:
a. Twist each strip and place it on the prepared baking sheet, leaving some space between each.
b. Bake in the preheated oven for 15-20 minutes or until the elephant ears are golden brown and puffed up.
7. Cool and Dust (Optional):
Allow the elephant ears to cool on a wire rack. If desired, dust with powdered sugar for an extra touch of sweetness.

Nutrition Information:
Note: Nutrition information is approximate and may vary based on specific ingredients and serving sizes.
- Serving Size: 1 elephant ear pastry
- Calories: 180
- Total Fat: 11g
- Saturated Fat: 6g
- Trans Fat: 0g
- Cholesterol: 20mg

- Sodium: 85mg
- Total Carbohydrates: 20g
- Dietary Fiber: 1g
- Sugars: 12g
- Protein: 1g

Embark on a culinary journey inspired by Jumanji with these Elephant Ear Pastries, perfect for sharing and savoring the magic of the jungle!

8. Python Pesto Pasta

Transport yourself into the heart of the Jumanji jungle with this exotic and flavorful Python Pesto Pasta. Inspired by the wild and unpredictable nature of the Jumanji film, this dish combines the adventurous spirit of the game with the comfort of a classic pasta dish. Embrace the unexpected and embark on a culinary journey with every bite.

Serving: 4 servings
Preparation Time: 15 minutes
Ready Time: 30 minutes

Ingredients:
- 1 lb python meat, thinly sliced
- 16 oz pasta of your choice
- 1 cup fresh basil leaves
- 1/2 cup grated Parmesan cheese
- 1/3 cup pine nuts
- 2 cloves garlic, minced
- 1/2 cup extra virgin olive oil
- Salt and pepper to taste
- Grated zest of 1 lemon
- 1/2 cup cherry tomatoes, halved (for garnish)
- Fresh basil leaves (for garnish)
- Grated Parmesan cheese (for serving)

Instructions:
1. Prepare the Python Meat:
- In a skillet over medium heat, cook the thinly sliced python meat until fully cooked. Season with salt and pepper to taste. Set aside.

2. Cook the Pasta:
- Cook the pasta according to the package instructions until al dente. Drain and set aside.

3. Prepare the Pesto Sauce:
- In a food processor, combine the fresh basil, grated Parmesan cheese, pine nuts, minced garlic, and lemon zest. Pulse until coarsely chopped.
- With the food processor running, gradually add the olive oil until the pesto reaches a smooth consistency. Season with salt and pepper to taste.

4. Combine Pasta and Pesto:
- In a large mixing bowl, toss the cooked pasta with the prepared pesto sauce until evenly coated.

5. Add Python Meat:
- Gently fold in the cooked python meat, ensuring it is distributed throughout the pasta.

6. Garnish and Serve:
- Plate the Python Pesto Pasta and garnish with halved cherry tomatoes, fresh basil leaves, and additional grated Parmesan cheese.

7. Serve:
- Serve immediately, allowing the flavors to meld together for a truly wild dining experience.

Nutrition Information:
Note: Nutritional values are approximate and may vary based on specific ingredients used.
- Calories per serving: 600
- Protein: 25g
- Carbohydrates: 45g
- Fat: 35g
- Fiber: 4g
- Sugar: 2g
- Sodium: 350mg

Dive into the untamed world of Jumanji with this Python Pesto Pasta—a dish that brings together the thrill of the jungle with the comfort of a classic Italian meal.

9. Zebra Striped Cupcakes

Step into the wild and adventurous world of Jumanji with these delightful Zebra Striped Cupcakes. Inspired by the unpredictable and whimsical nature of the Jumanji film, these cupcakes are a visual feast and a treat for the taste buds. The contrasting layers mimic the patterns of a zebra, adding a touch of the jungle to your dessert table. Get ready to embark on a flavorful journey with each bite!

Serving: Makes 12 cupcakes.
Preparation Time: 20 minutes.
Ready Time: 45 minutes.

Ingredients:
- 1 ½ cups all-purpose flour
- 1 ½ teaspoons baking powder
- ¼ teaspoon baking soda
- ¼ teaspoon salt
- ½ cup unsalted butter, softened
- 1 cup granulated sugar
- 2 large eggs
- 1 teaspoon vanilla extract
- 1 cup buttermilk
- 2 tablespoons cocoa powder
- Black food coloring gel

Instructions:
1. Preheat the Oven:
Preheat your oven to 350°F (180°C). Line a cupcake tin with paper liners.
2. Prepare the Dry Ingredients:
In a bowl, whisk together the flour, baking powder, baking soda, and salt. Set aside.
3. Cream the Butter and Sugar:
In a large mixing bowl, cream together the softened butter and sugar until light and fluffy.
4. Add Eggs and Vanilla:
Add the eggs one at a time, beating well after each addition. Stir in the vanilla extract.
5. Alternate Dry Ingredients and Buttermilk:

Gradually add the dry ingredients to the wet ingredients, alternating with buttermilk. Begin and end with the dry ingredients. Mix until just combined.

6. Divide the Batter:

Divide the batter into two equal parts.

7. Add Cocoa Powder and Coloring:

To one part of the batter, sift in the cocoa powder and add black food coloring gel. Mix until the batter turns a rich chocolate color.

8. Create Zebra Stripes:

Spoon a tablespoon of the vanilla batter into the center of each cupcake liner. On top of that, add a tablespoon of the chocolate batter. Continue alternating until each liner is filled about 2/3 full.

9. Swirl the Batter:

Using a toothpick or skewer, gently swirl the two batters together to create a zebra stripe pattern.

10. Bake:

Bake in the preheated oven for 18-20 minutes or until a toothpick inserted into the center comes out clean.

11. Cool:

Allow the cupcakes to cool in the tin for 5 minutes before transferring them to a wire rack to cool completely.

Nutrition Information:
(Per Cupcake)
- Calories: 220
- Total Fat: 10g
- Saturated Fat: 6g
- Cholesterol: 55mg
- Sodium: 180mg
- Total Carbohydrates: 29g
- Dietary Fiber: 1g
- Sugars: 18g
- Protein: 3g

Enjoy these Jumanji-inspired Zebra Striped Cupcakes that bring the magic of the jungle right to your dessert table!

10. Crocodile Kebabs

Embark on a culinary adventure inspired by the untamed spirit of Jumanji with these exotic Crocodile Kebabs. Transport your taste buds to the heart of the jungle as you savor the unique flavors and textures of this extraordinary dish. A perfect blend of adventure and gastronomy, these kebabs promise to tantalize your senses and transport you to the mysterious world of Jumanji.

Serving: 4 servings
Preparation Time: 30 minutes
Ready Time: 2 hours (including marination time)

Ingredients:
- 1 pound crocodile meat, cubed
- 1/4 cup olive oil
- 2 tablespoons lemon juice
- 2 cloves garlic, minced
- 1 teaspoon ground cumin
- 1 teaspoon smoked paprika
- 1 teaspoon dried oregano
- Salt and pepper, to taste
- Bell peppers, cherry tomatoes, and red onion chunks for skewering

Instructions:
1. In a bowl, whisk together olive oil, lemon juice, minced garlic, cumin, smoked paprika, dried oregano, salt, and pepper to create the marinade.
2. Add the crocodile meat cubes to the marinade, ensuring each piece is well-coated. Cover the bowl and refrigerate for at least 1-2 hours, allowing the flavors to meld and the meat to tenderize.
3. Preheat the grill to medium-high heat.
4. Thread the marinated crocodile meat onto skewers, alternating with bell peppers, cherry tomatoes, and red onion chunks.
5. Place the kebabs on the preheated grill and cook for 8-10 minutes, turning occasionally, until the crocodile meat is cooked through and has a delicious char.
6. Remove the kebabs from the grill and let them rest for a few minutes before serving.

Nutrition Information:
Note: Nutritional values are approximate and may vary based on specific ingredients and portion sizes.

- Calories: 250 per serving
- Protein: 25g
- Fat: 12g
- Carbohydrates: 8g
- Fiber: 2g
- Sugar: 3g
- Sodium: 400mg

Savor the thrill of the jungle with these Crocodile Kebabs, a dish that pays homage to the wild and unpredictable world of Jumanji. Gather your fellow adventurers and embark on a culinary journey that brings the essence of the game to your table.

11. Waterfall Smoothie Bowl

Embark on a culinary adventure inspired by the enchanting world of Jumanji with our delightful "Waterfall Smoothie Bowl." This vibrant and refreshing dish pays homage to the lush landscapes and thrilling escapades of the film. Immerse yourself in the flavors of the jungle as you savor this nutrient-packed bowl that brings a touch of magic to your breakfast or snack time.

Serving: 2 bowls
Preparation Time: 15 minutes
Ready Time: 15 minutes

Ingredients:
- 2 frozen bananas
- 1 cup frozen mixed berries (strawberries, blueberries, raspberries)
- 1/2 cup spinach leaves, washed
- 1/2 cup pineapple chunks, fresh or frozen
- 1/2 cup coconut water
- 1 tablespoon chia seeds
- 1 tablespoon honey or maple syrup (optional, for sweetness)
- Fresh fruits and edible flowers for garnish

Instructions:
1. Prepare the Base:

- In a blender, combine the frozen bananas, mixed berries, spinach, pineapple chunks, and coconut water.
- Blend until smooth and creamy. Add honey or maple syrup if additional sweetness is desired.

2. Create the Waterfall Effect:
- Pour the smoothie into two bowls, creating a swirling pattern to mimic the flow of a waterfall.

3. Add Texture:
- Sprinkle chia seeds over the smoothie surface for added texture and a nutritional boost.

4. Garnish:
- Decorate the smoothie bowl with fresh slices of tropical fruits, such as kiwi, mango, or passion fruit. Add edible flowers for a touch of whimsy.

5. Serve:
- Present your Waterfall Smoothie Bowl to your fellow adventurers and relish the flavors of Jumanji together.

Nutrition Information (per serving):
- Calories: 250
- Protein: 5g
- Fat: 2g
- Carbohydrates: 60g
- Fiber: 10g
- Sugar: 35g
- Vitamin C: 80mg
- Iron: 2mg

Indulge in this vibrant and nutritious Waterfall Smoothie Bowl as you embark on your own Jumanji-inspired culinary journey. May your taste buds be as adventurous as the game itself!

12. Quicksand Quinoa Bowl

Embark on a culinary adventure inspired by the thrilling world of Jumanji with our "Quicksand Quinoa Bowl." Just like the unpredictable challenges of the game, this bowl promises a flavorful journey through a mix of wholesome ingredients. Packed with the goodness of quinoa, fresh vegetables, and a hint of exotic spices, it's a dish that captures the essence of Jumanji's wild and exciting landscapes.

Serving: 4 servings
Preparation Time: 15 minutes
Ready Time: 30 minutes

Ingredients:
- 1 cup quinoa, rinsed and drained
- 2 cups vegetable broth
- 1 tablespoon olive oil
- 1 onion, finely chopped
- 2 cloves garlic, minced
- 1 red bell pepper, diced
- 1 yellow bell pepper, diced
- 1 zucchini, sliced
- 1 cup cherry tomatoes, halved
- 1 cup black beans, drained and rinsed
- 1 teaspoon ground cumin
- 1 teaspoon smoked paprika
- Salt and pepper to taste
- Fresh cilantro for garnish

Instructions:
1. In a medium-sized saucepan, combine quinoa and vegetable broth. Bring to a boil, then reduce heat to low, cover, and simmer for 15-20 minutes or until quinoa is cooked and liquid is absorbed.
2. While the quinoa is cooking, heat olive oil in a large skillet over medium heat. Add chopped onion and garlic, sautéing until fragrant and translucent.
3. Add diced red and yellow bell peppers, zucchini, cherry tomatoes, and black beans to the skillet. Cook for 5-7 minutes, or until the vegetables are tender yet still crisp.
4. Once the quinoa is ready, fluff it with a fork and add it to the skillet with the sautéed vegetables.
5. Sprinkle ground cumin, smoked paprika, salt, and pepper over the mixture. Stir well to ensure even distribution of the spices.
6. Allow the ingredients to meld together for an additional 2-3 minutes, letting the flavors combine.
7. Serve the Quicksand Quinoa Bowl hot, garnished with fresh cilantro.

Nutrition Information (per serving):

- Calories: 320
- Protein: 12g
- Carbohydrates: 54g
- Fiber: 10g
- Fat: 7g
- Saturated Fat: 1g
- Cholesterol: 0mg
- Sodium: 650mg

Dive into the Quicksand Quinoa Bowl, a dish inspired by Jumanji, and savor the harmony of flavors reminiscent of a journey through the untamed jungle.

13. Rhino Ravioli

In the heart of the Jumanji jungle lies a culinary adventure waiting to be discovered - Rhino Ravioli. Inspired by the majestic and powerful creatures that roam this fantastical land, these ravioli bring together robust flavors and textures reminiscent of the wilderness. Embrace the spirit of adventure and indulge in this flavorful dish that pays homage to the untamed wilderness of Jumanji.

Serving: This recipe serves 4 hungry adventurers.
Preparation Time: Preparation takes approximately 45 minutes.
Ready Time: Allow for approximately 1 hour and 15 minutes in total for preparation and cooking.

Ingredients:
For the Pasta Dough:
- 2 cups all-purpose flour
- 3 large eggs
- 1 tablespoon olive oil
- Pinch of salt

For the Filling:
- 1 pound ground beef
- 1/2 cup finely chopped onions
- 2 cloves garlic, minced
- 1/2 cup grated Parmesan cheese
- 1/4 cup chopped fresh parsley

- Salt and pepper to taste
For the Sauce:
- 2 tablespoons olive oil
- 3 cloves garlic, minced
- 1 can (28 ounces) crushed tomatoes
- 1 teaspoon dried oregano
- Salt and pepper to taste

Instructions:
1. Prepare the Pasta Dough:
- On a clean surface, make a mound with the flour and create a well in the center.
- Crack the eggs into the well, add olive oil, and a pinch of salt.
- Gradually mix the eggs and flour together until a dough forms.
- Knead the dough for about 8-10 minutes until it becomes smooth and elastic. Wrap it in plastic wrap and let it rest for 30 minutes.
2. Make the Filling:
- In a skillet over medium heat, cook the ground beef until browned. Add onions and garlic, cooking until onions are translucent.
- Remove from heat and stir in Parmesan cheese, parsley, salt, and pepper. Set aside to cool.
3. Roll Out the Dough:
- After resting, divide the dough into smaller portions. Roll each portion out thinly with a rolling pin or pasta machine.
- Place small spoonfuls of the filling on one sheet of dough, leaving space between each mound.
4. Assemble the Ravioli:
- Gently place another sheet of pasta over the one with the filling. Press around each mound of filling to seal the ravioli.
- Use a knife or a ravioli cutter to cut the individual ravioli squares.
5. Prepare the Sauce:
- In a saucepan, heat olive oil over medium heat. Add minced garlic and sauté until fragrant.
- Pour in the crushed tomatoes, add oregano, salt, and pepper. Simmer for about 15-20 minutes.
6. Cook the Ravioli:
- Bring a large pot of salted water to a boil. Gently drop the ravioli in batches and cook for 2-3 minutes or until they float to the top.
- Remove the cooked ravioli with a slotted spoon and place them into the tomato sauce. Gently toss to coat.

7. Serve:
- Plate the Rhino Ravioli, spooning extra sauce over the top. Garnish with additional Parmesan cheese and parsley if desired.

Nutrition Information:
(Note: Nutritional information can vary based on specific ingredients and portion sizes used in preparation. The following is an approximate estimation per serving.)
- Calories: 550
- Total Fat: 21g
- Saturated Fat: 7g
- Cholesterol: 175mg
- Sodium: 480mg
- Total Carbohydrate: 56g
- Dietary Fiber: 4g
- Sugars: 6g
- Protein: 32g

14. Baboon Banana Bread

Transport yourself into the wild world of Jumanji with this Baboon Banana Bread, inspired by the mischievous baboons in the film. This delectable treat is a fusion of flavors, combining the sweetness of ripe bananas with a hint of adventure. Gather your ingredients and embark on a culinary journey fit for an explorer!

Serving: Serves: 8-10
Slice into thick portions and serve warm or at room temperature for a delightful snack or dessert.
Preparation time: 15 minutes
Ready time: 1 hour 15 minutes (including baking)

Ingredients:
- 3 ripe bananas, mashed
- 1/2 cup unsalted butter, melted
- 3/4 cup granulated sugar
- 1 large egg, beaten
- 1 teaspoon vanilla extract

- 1 1/2 cups all-purpose flour
- 1 teaspoon baking soda
- 1/4 teaspoon salt
- 1/2 teaspoon ground cinnamon
- 1/4 teaspoon ground nutmeg
- 1/2 cup chopped walnuts or pecans (optional)

Instructions:
1. Preheat your oven to 350°F (175°C). Grease a 9x5-inch loaf pan or line it with parchment paper.
2. In a mixing bowl, mash the ripe bananas using a fork until smooth.
3. Stir in the melted butter and mix well. Add the granulated sugar, beaten egg, and vanilla extract. Combine until smooth.
4. In a separate bowl, whisk together the flour, baking soda, salt, cinnamon, and nutmeg.
5. Gradually add the dry ingredients to the banana mixture, stirring until just combined. Be careful not to overmix.
6. If using nuts, fold in the chopped walnuts or pecans into the batter.
7. Pour the batter into the prepared loaf pan, spreading it evenly.
8. Bake in the preheated oven for 60-70 minutes or until a toothpick inserted into the center comes out clean.
9. Once baked, remove the bread from the oven and allow it to cool in the pan for about 10-15 minutes.
10. Transfer the bread to a wire rack to cool completely before slicing.

Nutrition Information (per serving, assuming 10 servings):
- Calories: 270
- Total Fat: 12g
- Saturated Fat: 6g
- Cholesterol: 45mg
- Sodium: 260mg
- Total Carbohydrate: 38g
- Dietary Fiber: 2g
- Sugars: 20g
- Protein: 4g

Enjoy your Baboon Banana Bread, a delightful homage to the adventurous spirit of Jumanji!

15. Mangrove Sushi Rolls

Embark on a culinary adventure inspired by the captivating world of Jumanji with these Mangrove Sushi Rolls! As exotic as the landscapes and as thrilling as the quests within the film, these rolls bring together the vibrant flavors of the mangrove forests. Combining the freshness of seafood with the crunch of veggies, these sushi rolls will transport your taste buds on a wild journey.

Serving: Makes 4-6 servings
Preparation Time: 25 minutes
Ready Time: 35 minutes

Ingredients:
For the Sushi Rice:
- 2 cups sushi rice
- 2 1/2 cups water
- 1/3 cup rice vinegar
- 2 tablespoons sugar
- 1 teaspoon salt

For the Filling:
- 1/2 pound fresh shrimp, cooked and peeled
- 1/2 pound fresh crab meat, flaked
- 1 ripe avocado, thinly sliced
- 1 cucumber, julienned
- 4-6 nori seaweed sheets
- Soy sauce, for serving
- Pickled ginger, for serving
- Wasabi, for serving

Instructions:
1. Rinse the sushi rice in a fine-mesh sieve until the water runs clear. Combine the rice and water in a rice cooker and cook according to the manufacturer's instructions. Alternatively, cook the rice in a pot on the stove, following the package instructions.
2. While the rice cooks, in a small saucepan, heat the rice vinegar, sugar, and salt over low heat until the sugar dissolves. Set aside to cool.
3. Once the rice is cooked, transfer it to a large bowl. Gradually add the vinegar mixture to the rice, gently folding it in using a spatula. Be careful not to mash the rice. Let the rice cool to room temperature.

4. Place a sheet of nori on a bamboo sushi mat or a clean kitchen towel. With moistened hands, spread a thin layer of sushi rice evenly over the nori, leaving a small border at the top edge.
5. Arrange the shrimp, crab meat, avocado slices, and cucumber strips in the center of the rice-covered nori sheet.
6. Carefully roll the sushi using the bamboo mat or towel, applying gentle pressure to ensure a tight roll. Moisten the top border of the nori sheet with a little water to seal the roll.
7. Repeat the process with the remaining nori sheets and fillings.
8. Using a sharp knife, slice each roll into 6-8 pieces.
9. Serve the Mangrove Sushi Rolls with soy sauce, pickled ginger, and wasabi on the side.

Nutrition Information (per serving):
(Note: Nutritional values may vary based on specific ingredients used)
Calories: 380
Total Fat: 5g
Saturated Fat: 1g
Cholesterol: 85mg
Sodium: 700mg
Total Carbohydrate: 70g
Dietary Fiber: 6g
Sugars: 4g
Protein: 15g
These Mangrove Sushi Rolls offer a delightful combination of flavors and textures that pay homage to the adventurous spirit of Jumanji. Enjoy these rolls as a tasty snack or part of a themed feast that transports you into the heart of the jungle!

16. Lion's Mane Mushroom Risotto

Step into the magical world of Jumanji with this delightful Lion's Mane Mushroom Risotto, inspired by the lush and mysterious landscapes of the film. Just like the unpredictable twists and turns in the game, this dish offers a unique blend of flavors and textures. Lion's Mane mushrooms, known for their distinctive appearance and rich umami taste, take center stage in this risotto, creating a dish that is both comforting and adventurous.

Serving: 4 servings
Preparation Time: 15 minutes
Ready Time: 40 minutes

Ingredients:
- 1 1/2 cups Arborio rice
- 1 cup Lion's Mane mushrooms, finely chopped
- 1/2 cup dry white wine
- 4 cups vegetable broth, kept warm
- 1 small onion, finely chopped
- 2 cloves garlic, minced
- 1/2 cup Parmesan cheese, grated
- 2 tablespoons olive oil
- 1 tablespoon unsalted butter
- Salt and black pepper to taste
- Fresh parsley, chopped (for garnish)

Instructions:
1. Prepare the Mushroom Mixture:
- In a large pan, heat 1 tablespoon of olive oil over medium heat.
- Add the finely chopped Lion's Mane mushrooms and sauté until they release their moisture and turn golden brown, about 5-7 minutes. Set aside.
2. Sauté Onions and Garlic:
- In the same pan, add another tablespoon of olive oil.
- Sauté the chopped onion and garlic until they become translucent, about 3-5 minutes.
3. Toast the Rice:
- Add Arborio rice to the pan and stir to coat it with the oil, toasting it for 2-3 minutes until the edges become translucent.
4. Deglaze with Wine:
- Pour in the white wine and stir until the liquid is mostly absorbed.
5. Cook the Risotto:
- Begin adding the warm vegetable broth one ladle at a time, stirring frequently. Allow the liquid to be absorbed before adding the next ladle.
6. Incorporate Mushroom Mixture:
- After about 10 minutes of cooking, add the sautéed Lion's Mane mushrooms to the risotto, continuing to add broth until the rice is creamy and cooked to al dente texture.

7. Finish with Cheese and Butter:
- Stir in the grated Parmesan cheese and unsalted butter, ensuring a creamy and velvety consistency.
8. Season and Garnish:
- Season the risotto with salt and black pepper to taste. Garnish with freshly chopped parsley.
9. Serve:
- Spoon the Lion's Mane Mushroom Risotto onto plates, serving it hot and garnished with additional Parmesan cheese and parsley if desired.

Nutrition Information:
(Per serving)
- Calories: 380
- Protein: 8g
- Carbohydrates: 60g
- Fat: 12g
- Fiber: 3g

Immerse yourself in the enchanting flavors of Jumanji with this Lion's Mane Mushroom Risotto—a dish that captures the essence of the wild and the wonderful. Enjoy the journey!

17. Tarzan Tiramisu

Transport your taste buds to the heart of the jungle with the "Tarzan Tiramisu," a delightful dessert inspired by the adventurous spirit of the film Jumanji. This tantalizing treat combines the richness of traditional tiramisu with a playful twist, making it the perfect sweet finale to your cinematic feast. Get ready to embark on a flavor journey that mirrors the excitement of the game itself!

Serving: Serves 8
Preparation Time: 20 minutes
Ready Time: 4 hours (includes chilling time)

Ingredients:
- 1 cup strong brewed coffee, cooled
- 3 tablespoons coffee liqueur (e.g., Kahlúa)
- 3 large eggs, separated

- 3/4 cup granulated sugar
- 1 cup mascarpone cheese, softened
- 1 cup heavy cream
- 1 teaspoon vanilla extract
- 24 to 30 ladyfinger cookies
- Cocoa powder, for dusting
- Chocolate shavings, for garnish (optional)

Instructions:
1. Brew the Coffee:
- Prepare a cup of strong brewed coffee and allow it to cool. Stir in the coffee liqueur and set aside.
2. Separate Eggs:
- Separate the egg yolks from the whites into two different bowls.
3. Prepare Egg Yolks Mixture:
- In a bowl with the egg yolks, add half of the granulated sugar. Whisk until the mixture is pale and creamy. Fold in the mascarpone cheese until smooth.
4. Whip the Egg Whites:
- In a separate bowl, whip the egg whites until soft peaks form. Gradually add the remaining sugar and continue to whip until stiff peaks form.
5. Combine Egg Mixtures:
- Gently fold the whipped egg whites into the mascarpone mixture until well combined.
6. Whip the Cream:
- In another bowl, whip the heavy cream and vanilla extract until stiff peaks form.
7. Combine Cream and Mascarpone Mixtures:
- Fold the whipped cream into the mascarpone mixture until smooth and well incorporated.
8. Assemble the Tarzan Tiramisu:
- Quickly dip each ladyfinger into the coffee mixture, ensuring they are coated but not soggy. Arrange a layer of dipped ladyfingers in the bottom of a serving dish.
- Spread half of the mascarpone mixture over the ladyfingers. Repeat with another layer of dipped ladyfingers and the remaining mascarpone mixture.
- Cover and refrigerate for at least 4 hours, allowing the flavors to meld and the tiramisu to set.
9. Finish and Garnish:

- Before serving, dust the top of the tiramisu with cocoa powder and garnish with chocolate shavings if desired.

Nutrition Information:
- (Per Serving - 1/8 of recipe)
- Calories: 380
- Total Fat: 28g
- Saturated Fat: 16g
- Trans Fat: 0g
- Cholesterol: 150mg
- Sodium: 60mg
- Total Carbohydrates: 26g
- Dietary Fiber: 0g
- Sugars: 14g
- Protein: 5g

Indulge in the Tarzan Tiramisu, and let the flavors of this Jumanji-inspired dessert whisk you away on a culinary adventure!

18. Ostrich Omelette

Step into the wild and embark on a culinary adventure inspired by the enchanting world of Jumanji! Our "Ostrich Omelette" is a tribute to the exotic and untamed spirit of the jungle. Just like the unpredictable twists and turns of the Jumanji game, this omelette promises a delightful surprise with every bite. Prepare to tantalize your taste buds with the rich and lean flavors of ostrich meat, creating an omelette that's both unique and delicious.

Serving: Serves 2
Preparation Time: 15 minutes
Ready Time: 25 minutes

Ingredients:
- 4 large ostrich eggs
- 1/2 cup diced ostrich meat
- 1/4 cup diced red bell pepper
- 1/4 cup diced green bell pepper
- 1/4 cup diced red onion

- 1/4 cup shredded cheddar cheese
- 2 tablespoons chopped fresh parsley
- Salt and pepper to taste
- 2 tablespoons olive oil

Instructions:
1. Preheat: Heat olive oil in a non-stick skillet over medium heat.
2. Sauté Vegetables: Add diced red bell pepper, green bell pepper, and red onion to the skillet. Sauté until vegetables are tender, about 3-5 minutes.
3. Cook Ostrich Meat: Add diced ostrich meat to the skillet with the sautéed vegetables. Cook until the ostrich meat is browned, approximately 5-7 minutes. Season with salt and pepper to taste.
4. Whisk Ostrich Eggs: In a bowl, whisk the ostrich eggs until well combined. Pour the eggs into the skillet with the cooked vegetables and ostrich meat.
5. Add Cheese and Parsley: Sprinkle shredded cheddar cheese and chopped fresh parsley over the eggs in the skillet.
6. Cook Omelette: Allow the omelette to cook undisturbed for a few minutes until the edges begin to set. Gently lift the edges with a spatula to let the uncooked eggs flow underneath. Continue until the omelette is mostly set.
7. Fold and Serve: Once the omelette is cooked to your liking, carefully fold it in half with the spatula. Slide the omelette onto a plate.
8. Garnish and Enjoy: Garnish with additional parsley if desired. Serve hot and enjoy your Jumanji-inspired Ostrich Omelette!

Nutrition Information:
Note: Nutrition values are approximate and may vary based on specific ingredients used.
- Calories per serving: 320 kcal
- Protein: 28g
- Carbohydrates: 5g
- Fat: 20g
- Fiber: 1g
- Sugar: 2g
- Sodium: 450mg

Embark on this culinary journey inspired by the magic of Jumanji, and let the Ostrich Omelette transport you to a world of bold flavors and exotic ingredients!

19. Rockslide Rockfish

Embark on a culinary adventure inspired by the untamed wilderness of Jumanji with our Rockslide Rockfish recipe. Just like the thrilling twists and turns in the Jumanji films, this dish is an exciting combination of flavors that will transport your taste buds to a world of bold spices and succulent seafood. The name itself evokes images of rocky landscapes and adventurous encounters, making it a perfect addition to your Jumanji-inspired feast.

Serving: 4 servings
Preparation Time: 15 minutes
Ready Time: 35 minutes

Ingredients:
- 4 rockfish fillets (about 6 ounces each)
- 1 cup breadcrumbs
- 1/2 cup grated Parmesan cheese
- 1 tablespoon dried oregano
- 1 tablespoon paprika
- 1 teaspoon garlic powder
- 1 teaspoon onion powder
- Salt and black pepper to taste
- 1/2 cup melted butter
- 1 lemon, sliced for garnish
- Fresh parsley, chopped for garnish

Instructions:
1. Preheat the Oven:
Preheat your oven to 375°F (190°C).
2. Prepare the Breading Mixture:
In a shallow bowl, combine the breadcrumbs, grated Parmesan cheese, dried oregano, paprika, garlic powder, onion powder, salt, and black pepper. Mix well to ensure an even distribution of flavors.
3. Coat the Rockfish:

Dip each rockfish fillet into the melted butter, making sure it is fully coated. Then, dredge the fillets in the breadcrumb mixture, pressing gently to adhere the coating to the fish.

4. Arrange on a Baking Sheet:

Place the breaded rockfish fillets on a greased or parchment-lined baking sheet, ensuring they are not touching each other.

5. Bake to Perfection:

Bake in the preheated oven for 20-25 minutes or until the rockfish is cooked through and the coating is golden brown and crispy.

6. Garnish and Serve:

Remove the rockfish from the oven and garnish with fresh lemon slices and chopped parsley. Serve hot and savor the adventure-infused flavors of Rockslide Rockfish.

Nutrition Information:

(Per serving)
- Calories: 380 kcal
- Protein: 28g
- Fat: 22g
- Carbohydrates: 18g
- Fiber: 2g
- Sugars: 2g
- Sodium: 620mg

Immerse yourself in the world of Jumanji with this delectable Rockslide Rockfish dish, perfect for a family dinner or a themed gathering with friends. Let the flavors take you on a wild journey, just like the iconic game itself!

20. Gecko Gingerbread Cookies

Transport yourself into the magical world of Jumanji with these delightful Gecko Gingerbread Cookies. Inspired by the enchanting creatures that roam the jungle, these cookies are a perfect blend of sweet and spicy, creating a flavor adventure reminiscent of the film. Get ready to embark on a culinary journey that combines the magic of Jumanji with the joy of homemade gingerbread cookies.

Serving: Makes approximately 24 Gecko Gingerbread Cookies.

Preparation Time: 20 minutes
Ready Time: 2 hours (includes chilling time)

Ingredients:
- 3 cups all-purpose flour
- 1 teaspoon baking soda
- 1/2 teaspoon baking powder
- 1/2 teaspoon salt
- 1 tablespoon ground ginger
- 1 tablespoon ground cinnamon
- 1/2 teaspoon ground nutmeg
- 1/2 teaspoon ground cloves
- 3/4 cup unsalted butter, softened
- 1 cup brown sugar, packed
- 1 large egg
- 1/2 cup molasses
- 1 teaspoon vanilla extract
- Gecko-shaped cookie cutter

Instructions:
1. In a medium bowl, whisk together the flour, baking soda, baking powder, salt, ginger, cinnamon, nutmeg, and cloves. Set aside.
2. In a large mixing bowl, cream together the softened butter and brown sugar until light and fluffy.
3. Add the egg to the butter and sugar mixture, beating well after each addition. Then, mix in the molasses and vanilla extract until well combined.
4. Gradually add the dry ingredients to the wet ingredients, mixing until a soft dough forms. Divide the dough in half, wrap each portion in plastic wrap, and refrigerate for at least 1 hour or until firm.
5. Preheat the oven to 350°F (175°C) and line baking sheets with parchment paper.
6. On a lightly floured surface, roll out one portion of the chilled dough to about 1/4 inch thickness. Use the gecko-shaped cookie cutter to cut out cookies, placing them on the prepared baking sheets.
7. Bake for 8-10 minutes or until the edges are lightly golden. Allow the cookies to cool on the baking sheets for a few minutes before transferring them to a wire rack to cool completely.
8. Repeat the rolling and cutting process with the remaining dough.

Nutrition Information:
(Per serving - 1 Gecko Gingerbread Cookie)
- Calories: 120
- Total Fat: 5g
- Saturated Fat: 3g
- Cholesterol: 18mg
- Sodium: 90mg
- Total Carbohydrates: 18g
- Dietary Fiber: 0.5g
- Sugars: 8g
- Protein: 1g

Embark on a culinary adventure with these Gecko Gingerbread Cookies and let the flavors of Jumanji fill your kitchen with warmth and magic.

21. Jaguar Jambalaya

Embark on a culinary adventure inspired by the wild and whimsical world of Jumanji with our Jaguar Jambalaya. This vibrant and flavorful dish pays homage to the thrill of the jungle and the unpredictable nature of the game. Just like the characters in Jumanji, you're in for a ride with every bite of this exotic and hearty Jambalaya.

Serving: 4-6 servings
Preparation Time: 20 minutes
Ready Time: 45 minutes

Ingredients:
- 1 lb (450g) boneless, skinless chicken thighs, cut into bite-sized pieces
- 1 lb (450g) smoked sausage, sliced
- 1 lb (450g) shrimp, peeled and deveined
- 1 large onion, finely chopped
- 1 bell pepper, diced
- 3 celery stalks, sliced
- 3 cloves garlic, minced
- 1 cup (200g) cherry tomatoes, halved
- 1 cup (200g) okra, sliced
- 1 cup (200g) long-grain white rice
- 3 cups (710ml) chicken broth

- 1 can (14 oz/400g) diced tomatoes, undrained
- 2 tablespoons Cajun seasoning
- 1 teaspoon dried thyme
- 1 teaspoon paprika
- Salt and black pepper to taste
- 2 tablespoons olive oil
- Fresh parsley for garnish

Instructions:
1. In a large, heavy-bottomed pot, heat olive oil over medium heat.
2. Add chicken pieces and cook until browned on all sides. Remove chicken from the pot and set aside.
3. In the same pot, add sliced sausage and cook until browned. Remove sausage and set aside.
4. Add chopped onion, bell pepper, celery, and minced garlic to the pot. Cook until the vegetables are softened.
5. Stir in rice, Cajun seasoning, thyme, paprika, salt, and black pepper. Cook for 2-3 minutes, allowing the rice to absorb the flavors.
6. Pour in chicken broth, diced tomatoes (with their juice), and return the cooked chicken and sausage to the pot. Bring to a simmer.
7. Cover the pot and let it simmer for 15-20 minutes, or until the rice is almost tender.
8. Add shrimp, cherry tomatoes, and sliced okra. Continue to simmer for an additional 5-7 minutes, or until the shrimp are cooked through.
9. Adjust seasoning to taste. Serve the Jaguar Jambalaya hot, garnished with fresh parsley.

Nutrition Information:
(Per Serving)
- Calories: 450
- Total Fat: 15g
- Saturated Fat: 4g
- Cholesterol: 150mg
- Sodium: 1100mg
- Total Carbohydrates: 45g
- Dietary Fiber: 4g
- Sugars: 5g
- Protein: 35g

Note: Nutrition information is approximate and may vary based on specific ingredients and portion sizes.

22. Coconut Cannonballs

Embark on a culinary adventure inspired by the wild and enchanting world of Jumanji with these delectable Coconut Cannonballs. These bite-sized treats are a nod to the thrilling scenes in the jungle, where surprises await at every turn. The combination of coconut and a hint of tropical sweetness will transport your taste buds to the heart of the mysterious board game. Get ready to roll these Coconut Cannonballs into your next movie night for a snack that's both delightful and daring.

Serving: Makes approximately 24 Coconut Cannonballs.
Preparation Time: 15 minutes
Ready Time: 2 hours (including chilling time)

Ingredients:
- 2 cups shredded coconut
- 1/2 cup sweetened condensed milk
- 1/4 cup powdered sugar
- 1/4 cup coconut oil, melted
- 1 teaspoon vanilla extract
- 1/2 teaspoon coconut extract (optional)
- 1/4 teaspoon salt
- 1 cup dark chocolate chips
- 1 tablespoon coconut oil (for chocolate coating)
- Crushed nuts or additional shredded coconut for coating (optional)

Instructions:
1. Mixing the Coconut Base:
- In a large bowl, combine shredded coconut, sweetened condensed milk, powdered sugar, melted coconut oil, vanilla extract, coconut extract (if using), and salt. Mix well until the ingredients are evenly combined.
2. Forming the Cannonballs:
- Scoop out tablespoon-sized portions of the coconut mixture and roll them into compact balls. Place the coconut balls on a parchment-lined tray.
3. Chilling:

- Place the tray in the refrigerator and let the coconut balls chill for at least 1 hour, or until firm.

4. Preparing the Chocolate Coating:
- In a microwave-safe bowl, melt the dark chocolate chips and 1 tablespoon of coconut oil in 30-second intervals, stirring between each interval until smooth.

5. Coating the Cannonballs:
- Take the chilled coconut balls and, using a fork, dip each one into the melted chocolate, ensuring they are fully coated. Allow any excess chocolate to drip off before placing them back on the parchment-lined tray.

6. Optional Toppings:
- While the chocolate is still wet, sprinkle crushed nuts or additional shredded coconut on top for added texture and flavor.

7. Setting the Chocolate:
- Place the tray back in the refrigerator and let the chocolate coating set for at least 1 hour or until firm.

8. Serve and Enjoy:
- Once the Coconut Cannonballs are fully set, transfer them to a serving plate. These delightful treats are now ready to be enjoyed during your Jumanji movie marathon!

Nutrition Information:
(Per Serving - 1 Coconut Cannonball)
- Calories: 120
- Total Fat: 8g
- Saturated Fat: 6g
- Trans Fat: 0g
- Cholesterol: 3mg
- Sodium: 40mg
- Total Carbohydrates: 12g
- Dietary Fiber: 1g
- Sugars: 9g
- Protein: 1g

Note: Nutrition information is approximate and may vary based on specific ingredients and quantities used.

23. Python Pizza

Embark on a culinary adventure inspired by the mystical world of Jumanji with our "Python Pizza" – a savory delight that captures the essence of the wild and unpredictable jungle. This pizza is a tribute to the film's adventurous spirit, featuring bold flavors and a unique combination of ingredients that will transport your taste buds to a realm of excitement. Don't be alarmed by the name; no snakes were harmed in the making of this pizza. Instead, we've crafted a delicious pie that pays homage to the film's thrilling atmosphere.

Serving: 4-6 people
Preparation Time: 15 minutes
Ready Time: 25 minutes

Ingredients:
- 1 pre-made pizza dough (store-bought or homemade)
- 1 cup tomato sauce
- 1 cup shredded mozzarella cheese
- 1/2 cup cooked and shredded chicken (python-inspired)
- 1/4 cup sliced black olives (for a touch of darkness)
- 1/4 cup sliced green bell peppers (jungle greenery)
- 1/4 cup sliced red onions (a hint of adventure)
- 1/4 cup sliced mushrooms (foraged from the wild)
- 1 teaspoon dried oregano
- 1 teaspoon garlic powder
- Olive oil for drizzling

Instructions:
1. Preheat your oven to 450°F (230°C).
2. Roll out the pizza dough on a floured surface to your desired thickness.
3. Transfer the rolled-out dough to a pizza stone or a baking sheet.
4. Spread a generous layer of tomato sauce over the dough, leaving a small border around the edges.
5. Sprinkle the shredded mozzarella cheese evenly over the sauce.
6. Evenly distribute the shredded chicken, black olives, green bell peppers, red onions, and mushrooms over the cheese.
7. Sprinkle dried oregano and garlic powder over the toppings for an extra burst of flavor.

8. Drizzle a bit of olive oil over the pizza for a golden crust.
9. Place the pizza in the preheated oven and bake for 15-20 minutes, or until the crust is golden and the cheese is bubbly and slightly browned.
10. Remove the pizza from the oven and let it cool for a few minutes before slicing.

Nutrition Information:
Note: Nutrition information may vary based on specific ingredients and portion sizes.
- Calories per serving: 300
- Total Fat: 12g
- Saturated Fat: 6g
- Cholesterol: 35mg
- Sodium: 600mg
- Total Carbohydrates: 30g
- Dietary Fiber: 2g
- Sugars: 3g
- Protein: 15g

This Python Pizza is not only a feast for the senses but also a culinary tribute to the fantastical world of Jumanji. Enjoy this delicious creation with friends and family as you embark on your own adventure in the realm of flavor!

24. Snakefruit Salad

Step into the world of Jumanji with this exotic Snakefruit Salad! Inspired by the lush and mysterious jungle setting of the film, this refreshing salad captures the essence of adventure in every bite. The vibrant colors and unique flavors of snake fruit, combined with crisp vegetables and a zesty dressing, create a dish that will transport you to the heart of the Jumanji jungle. Get ready for a culinary journey that mirrors the excitement of the game itself!

Serving: 4 servings
Preparation Time: 15 minutes
Ready Time: 20 minutes

Ingredients:

- 4 snake fruits, peeled and thinly sliced
- 2 cups mixed salad greens
- 1 cucumber, thinly sliced
- 1 bell pepper, thinly sliced (choose your preferred color)
- 1/2 red onion, thinly sliced
- 1/4 cup fresh cilantro, chopped
- 1/4 cup roasted peanuts, chopped

For the Dressing:
- 3 tablespoons olive oil
- 2 tablespoons soy sauce
- 1 tablespoon honey
- 1 tablespoon lime juice
- 1 teaspoon fresh ginger, grated
- 1 clove garlic, minced
- Salt and pepper to taste

Instructions:
1. In a large bowl, combine the snake fruit slices, mixed salad greens, cucumber, bell pepper, red onion, and cilantro.
2. In a small bowl, whisk together the olive oil, soy sauce, honey, lime juice, ginger, garlic, salt, and pepper to create the dressing.
3. Drizzle the dressing over the salad and toss gently to combine, ensuring the ingredients are evenly coated.
4. Sprinkle the chopped peanuts over the top for a delightful crunch.
5. Serve immediately and enjoy the unique flavors of the Jumanji-inspired Snakefruit Salad!

Nutrition Information:
(Per Serving)
- Calories: 220
- Total Fat: 14g
- Saturated Fat: 2g
- Trans Fat: 0g
- Cholesterol: 0mg
- Sodium: 400mg
- Total Carbohydrates: 22g
- Dietary Fiber: 4g
- Sugars: 14g
- Protein: 5g

Immerse yourself in the magic of Jumanji with this delectable Snakefruit Salad that brings the jungle to your plate!

25. Water Buffalo Wings

Embark on a culinary adventure inspired by the wild and unpredictable world of Jumanji with our tantalizing "Water Buffalo Wings." These wings pay homage to the mystical and exotic creatures that roam the Jumanji jungle, offering a flavorful experience that transcends the boundaries of ordinary cuisine. Get ready to unleash the magic onto your taste buds and recreate the excitement of the game in your kitchen!

Serving: 4 servings
Preparation Time: 15 minutes
Ready Time: 45 minutes

Ingredients:
- 2 lbs chicken wings, split at joints, tips discarded
- 1 cup buttermilk
- 1 cup all-purpose flour
- 1 tsp garlic powder
- 1 tsp onion powder
- 1 tsp smoked paprika
- 1/2 tsp cayenne pepper (adjust to taste)
- Salt and pepper to taste
- 1 cup buffalo wing sauce
- 1/2 cup unsalted butter, melted
- 1 tbsp honey
- 1 tbsp soy sauce
- Vegetable oil for frying
- Celery sticks and ranch dressing for serving

Instructions:
1. In a large bowl, marinate the chicken wings in buttermilk for at least 30 minutes. This helps to tenderize the meat and infuse it with flavor.
2. In a separate bowl, combine the flour, garlic powder, onion powder, smoked paprika, cayenne pepper, salt, and pepper.

3. Heat vegetable oil in a deep fryer or a large, deep skillet to 375°F (190°C).
4. Dredge the marinated wings in the flour mixture, ensuring they are evenly coated.
5. Fry the wings in batches for about 10-12 minutes or until golden brown and crispy. Ensure the internal temperature reaches 165°F (74°C).
6. While the wings are frying, mix the buffalo wing sauce, melted butter, honey, and soy sauce in a saucepan over medium heat. Stir until well combined.
7. Once the wings are cooked, transfer them to a large bowl. Pour the buffalo sauce mixture over the wings and toss until evenly coated.
8. Serve the Water Buffalo Wings hot with celery sticks and a side of ranch dressing.

Nutrition Information:
(Per Serving)
- Calories: 520 kcal
- Protein: 28g
- Fat: 35g
- Carbohydrates: 20g
- Fiber: 1g
- Sugar: 4g
- Sodium: 1250mg

Indulge in the magic of Jumanji with these Water Buffalo Wings, a dish that brings the spirit of the jungle right to your table. Enjoy the crunch, savor the spice, and let the adventure unfold in every bite!

26. Bazaar Banana Split

Transport yourself into the heart of Jumanji with the Bazaar Banana Split—a delightful treat inspired by the wild and whimsical world of the iconic film series. This indulgent dessert captures the spirit of adventure with a fusion of tropical flavors and a playful presentation. Get ready to embark on a culinary journey as you savor each bite of this Bazaar Banana Split, a tribute to the fantastical feasts of Jumanji.

Serving: Serves 4
Preparation Time: 15 minutes

Ready Time: 20 minutes

Ingredients:
- 4 ripe bananas
- 1 cup pineapple chunks, fresh or canned
- 1 cup strawberries, sliced
- 1 cup vanilla ice cream
- 1 cup chocolate ice cream
- 1 cup coconut ice cream
- 1/2 cup chopped nuts (walnuts or almonds)
- 1/2 cup chocolate sauce
- 1/2 cup caramel sauce
- Whipped cream for topping
- Maraschino cherries for garnish

Instructions:
1. Prepare the Bananas:
Peel and split the bananas in half lengthwise. Arrange them in a serving dish or on a banana split boat.
2. Add the Ice Cream:
Scoop generous portions of vanilla, chocolate, and coconut ice cream between the banana halves.
3. Top with Fruits:
Sprinkle pineapple chunks and sliced strawberries over the scoops of ice cream.
4. Drizzle with Sauces:
Drizzle chocolate sauce and caramel sauce over the entire banana split.
5. Crunchy Nut Topping:
Sprinkle chopped nuts evenly across the banana split for a delightful crunch.
6. Whipped Cream Crown:
Finish by adding a generous dollop of whipped cream on top of each ice cream scoop.
7. Cherry on Top:
Garnish with maraschino cherries for a classic touch.
8. Serve and Enjoy:
Serve immediately and relish the flavors of the Bazaar Banana Split. Don't forget to share this delightful dessert with your fellow Jumanji enthusiasts!

Nutrition Information (per serving):
(Note: Nutrition information is approximate and may vary based on specific ingredients and brands used.)
- Calories: 450
- Total Fat: 22g
- Saturated Fat: 10g
- Trans Fat: 0g
- Cholesterol: 45mg
- Sodium: 120mg
- Total Carbohydrates: 60g
- Dietary Fiber: 6g
- Sugars: 40g
- Protein: 7g

Embark on this culinary adventure inspired by Jumanji, and let the Bazaar Banana Split take your taste buds on a wild ride!

27. Monkey Magic Muffins

Embark on a culinary adventure inspired by the magical world of Jumanji with these delightful Monkey Magic Muffins. Just like the unpredictable and whimsical nature of the game itself, these muffins are a surprising blend of flavors and textures that will transport your taste buds to the heart of the jungle. Packed with nuts, bananas, and a touch of enchantment, these muffins are a tribute to the film's sense of wonder and excitement.

Serving: Makes 12 muffins.
Preparation Time: 15 minutes.
Ready Time: 35 minutes.

Ingredients:
- 2 ripe bananas, mashed
- 1/2 cup melted butter
- 1 teaspoon vanilla extract
- 1/2 cup sugar
- 1 large egg, beaten
- 1 1/2 cups all-purpose flour
- 1 teaspoon baking soda

- 1/2 teaspoon baking powder
- 1/4 teaspoon salt
- 1/2 cup chopped walnuts
- 1/2 cup chopped pecans
- 1/2 cup shredded coconut
- 1/2 cup chocolate chips
- Magic dust (a pinch of cinnamon and nutmeg)

Instructions:
1. Preheat your oven to 350°F (175°C). Grease a muffin tin or line it with paper liners.
2. In a large mixing bowl, combine the mashed bananas, melted butter, and vanilla extract. Mix well.
3. Add the sugar and beaten egg to the banana mixture, stirring until smooth.
4. In a separate bowl, whisk together the flour, baking soda, baking powder, and salt.
5. Gradually add the dry ingredients to the wet ingredients, mixing until just combined.
6. Fold in the chopped walnuts, pecans, shredded coconut, and chocolate chips.
7. Sprinkle the magic dust (cinnamon and nutmeg) into the batter and gently fold it in for an extra touch of enchantment.
8. Spoon the batter into the muffin cups, filling each about two-thirds full.
9. Bake in the preheated oven for 20-25 minutes or until a toothpick inserted into the center comes out clean.
10. Allow the Monkey Magic Muffins to cool in the tin for 5 minutes before transferring them to a wire rack to cool completely.

Nutrition Information:
(Per serving - 1 muffin)
- Calories: 240
- Total Fat: 14g
- Saturated Fat: 7g
- Trans Fat: 0g
- Cholesterol: 30mg
- Sodium: 180mg
- Total Carbohydrates: 28g
- Dietary Fiber: 2g

- Sugars: 14g
- Protein: 3g

Indulge in the magic of Jumanji with these whimsical Monkey Magic Muffins that capture the essence of the jungle and bring a sense of adventure to your plate.

28. Panther Pumpkin Soup

Step into the wild world of Jumanji with this exotic and hearty Panther Pumpkin Soup inspired by the mysterious and adventurous film series. Rich in flavors and textures, this soup is a tantalizing journey for your taste buds. The combination of the earthy pumpkin and the bold essence of the panther creates a culinary experience that mirrors the excitement of Jumanji itself.

Serving: 4 servings
Preparation Time: 15 minutes
Ready Time: 45 minutes

Ingredients:
- 1 medium-sized pumpkin, peeled and diced
- 1 pound panther meat, cubed (Note: Substitute with lean beef or venison if panther meat is unavailable)
- 1 large onion, finely chopped
- 3 cloves garlic, minced
- 2 carrots, peeled and sliced
- 2 celery stalks, chopped
- 1 tablespoon olive oil
- 6 cups vegetable or beef broth
- 1 teaspoon ground cumin
- 1 teaspoon smoked paprika
- 1/2 teaspoon cinnamon
- Salt and pepper to taste
- Fresh parsley for garnish

Instructions:
1. In a large pot, heat the olive oil over medium heat. Add the chopped onion and minced garlic, sautéing until the onions are translucent.

2. Add the panther meat cubes to the pot, cooking until browned on all sides. If you're using a substitute meat, ensure it is cooked through.
3. Stir in the diced pumpkin, sliced carrots, and chopped celery, allowing them to cook for 5 minutes to enhance their flavors.
4. Pour in the vegetable or beef broth, ensuring it covers all the ingredients. Bring the soup to a boil, then reduce the heat to simmer.
5. Add the ground cumin, smoked paprika, cinnamon, salt, and pepper. Let the soup simmer for 30-35 minutes or until the vegetables are tender and the flavors have melded.
6. Once cooked, use an immersion blender to puree the soup until smooth. Alternatively, transfer small batches to a blender and blend until smooth, then return to the pot.
7. Adjust seasoning to taste. Serve the Panther Pumpkin Soup hot, garnished with fresh parsley for a burst of color and added freshness.

Nutrition Information:
(Per serving)
- Calories: 280
- Protein: 18g
- Fat: 12g
- Carbohydrates: 25g
- Fiber: 6g
- Sugar: 8g
- Sodium: 900mg

Embark on this culinary adventure and savor the wild side of Jumanji with every spoonful of this Panther Pumpkin Soup!

29. Jungle Juice

Embark on a culinary adventure inspired by the wild and unpredictable world of Jumanji with our exhilarating Jungle Juice recipe. Just like the twists and turns in the iconic film, this vibrant concoction is a thrilling blend of flavors that will transport you to the heart of the jungle. Prepare to be enchanted by the fusion of exotic fruits and refreshing juices, creating a drink fit for explorers and adventurers alike.

Serving: Makes approximately 8 servings
Preparation Time: 15 minutes

Ready Time: 2 hours (including chilling time)

Ingredients:
- 2 cups pineapple juice
- 1 cup orange juice
- 1 cup mango juice
- 1 cup coconut water
- 1 cup passion fruit juice
- 1 cup guava nectar
- 1 cup white rum
- 1/2 cup dark rum
- 1/4 cup grenadine
- 1/4 cup lime juice
- Fresh fruit slices (pineapple, orange, mango) for garnish
- Ice cubes

Instructions:
1. Prepare the Jungle Mix:
In a large pitcher, combine pineapple juice, orange juice, mango juice, coconut water, passion fruit juice, guava nectar, white rum, dark rum, grenadine, and lime juice. Stir well to ensure all the flavors are combined.
2. Chill the Jungle Juice:
Place the pitcher in the refrigerator and let the jungle mix chill for at least 2 hours. This allows the flavors to meld together and creates a refreshing, cold beverage.
3. Serve with Style:
When ready to serve, fill glasses with ice cubes and pour the chilled Jungle Juice over the ice. Garnish each glass with fresh fruit slices, such as pineapple, orange, and mango, for a tropical touch.
4. Enjoy the Adventure:
Sip and savor the Jungle Juice, letting its exotic flavors transport you to the heart of Jumanji. Share this thrilling beverage with friends and family as you embark on your own culinary adventure.

Nutrition Information:
Note: Nutrition information is approximate and may vary based on specific ingredients used.
- Calories per serving: 180
- Total Fat: 0g
- Cholesterol: 0mg

- Sodium: 5mg
- Total Carbohydrates: 25g
- Dietary Fiber: 1g
- Sugars: 20g
- Protein: 1g

Dive into the wild with this Jungle Juice recipe, inspired by the magic and excitement of Jumanji. It's a taste of the unexpected, just like the game itself. Cheers to adventure and good company!

30. Elephant Eclair

Step into the magical world of Jumanji with this whimsical and delicious treat – the Elephant Eclair! Inspired by the larger-than-life adventures in the film, this dessert is sure to transport your taste buds to the heart of the jungle. With a rich and creamy filling, encased in a light, crispy pastry, the Elephant Eclair is a delightful homage to the wild wonders of Jumanji.

Serving: Makes 12 Elephant Eclairs.
Preparation Time: 30 minutes.
Ready Time: 2 hours (including chilling time).

Ingredients:
- 1 cup water
- 1/2 cup unsalted butter
- 1 cup all-purpose flour
- 4 large eggs
- 1 teaspoon vanilla extract

For the Filling:
- 2 cups heavy cream
- 1/2 cup powdered sugar
- 1 teaspoon vanilla extract

For the Chocolate Ganache:
- 1 cup semi-sweet chocolate chips
- 1/2 cup heavy cream

Optional:
- Edible gold dust for decoration

Instructions:
1. Prepare the Choux Pastry:
- In a saucepan, bring water and butter to a boil. Add flour and stir vigorously until the mixture forms a smooth ball.
- Remove from heat and let it cool for 5 minutes.
- Add eggs one at a time, beating well after each addition. Stir in vanilla extract.
- Transfer the dough to a piping bag fitted with a large round tip.
2. Shape the Elephant Eclairs:
- Preheat your oven to 400°F (200°C) and line a baking sheet with parchment paper.
- Pipe the dough onto the prepared baking sheet in the shape of elephant trunks and ears.
- Bake for 15-20 minutes or until golden brown and puffed. Allow them to cool completely.
3. Prepare the Filling:
- In a mixing bowl, whip the heavy cream, powdered sugar, and vanilla extract until stiff peaks form.
- Transfer the whipped cream into a piping bag.
4. Fill the Eclairs:
- Slice the cooled elephant trunks in half horizontally. Pipe or spoon the whipped cream onto the bottom half and cover with the top half.
5. Make the Chocolate Ganache:
- In a heatproof bowl, melt the chocolate chips and heavy cream together. Stir until smooth.
- Dip the top of each eclair into the chocolate ganache, allowing any excess to drip off.
6. Optional Decoration:
- If desired, sprinkle the eclairs with edible gold dust for a touch of Jumanji magic.
7. Chill and Serve:
- Place the filled and glazed eclairs in the refrigerator to set for at least an hour.
- Serve chilled and enjoy the wild and wonderful flavors inspired by Jumanji!

Nutrition Information:
Note: Nutritional values may vary based on specific ingredients and quantities used.
- Serving Size: 1 Elephant Eclair

- Calories: approximately 300
- Total Fat: 20g
- Saturated Fat: 12g
- Cholesterol: 100mg
- Sodium: 50mg
- Total Carbohydrates: 25g
- Dietary Fiber: 1g
- Sugars: 15g
- Protein: 4g

Indulge in the enchantment of Jumanji with these Elephant Eclairs, a delightful fusion of fantasy and flavor!

31. Tiger Tail Twizzlers

Step into the fantastical world of Jumanji with these delightful Tiger Tail Twizzlers! Inspired by the wild and whimsical creatures of the jungle, these sweet treats are not only visually captivating but also a delicious addition to your movie-inspired culinary adventure. Get ready to embark on a flavor journey that combines the essence of the jungle with the playful spirit of Jumanji.

Serving: Makes approximately 12 Tiger Tail Twizzlers
Preparation Time: 15 minutes
Ready Time: 2 hours (including chilling time)

Ingredients:
- 2 cups orange candy melts
- 1 cup black candy melts
- 1 tablespoon vegetable oil
- 1 teaspoon orange extract
- 1/2 teaspoon black licorice extract (optional)
- 12 long black licorice ropes

Instructions:
1. In separate microwave-safe bowls, melt the orange and black candy melts according to the package instructions.

2. Add vegetable oil to each melted candy, along with orange extract to the orange candy melts. If desired, add black licorice extract to the black candy melts for an extra layer of flavor.
3. Take a licorice rope and dip it into the melted orange candy, ensuring it's completely coated. Use a fork to remove any excess coating, allowing the excess to drip back into the bowl.
4. Place the coated licorice rope on a parchment-lined baking sheet and let it set for a few minutes.
5. Once the orange coating is set, drizzle the melted black candy over the orange-coated licorice ropes in a zig-zag pattern to create the tiger tail effect.
6. Place the Tiger Tail Twizzlers in the refrigerator for about 2 hours or until the candy coating is completely set.
7. Once set, carefully peel the twizzlers off the parchment paper and serve.

Nutrition Information (per serving):
- Calories: 120
- Total Fat: 6g
- Saturated Fat: 4g
- Trans Fat: 0g
- Cholesterol: 0mg
- Sodium: 20mg
- Total Carbohydrates: 18g
- Dietary Fiber: 0g
- Sugars: 15g
- Protein: 1g

Note: Nutrition information is approximate and may vary based on specific ingredients and quantities used.

32. Safari Sundae

Step into the wild with the "Safari Sundae," a delectable treat inspired by the adventurous world of Jumanji. This indulgent dessert is a delightful journey through layers of flavors, bringing the excitement of the jungle to your taste buds. Get ready for a taste adventure that's as wild and thrilling as the game itself.

Serving: Serves 4
Preparation Time: 15 minutes
Ready Time: 30 minutes

Ingredients:
- 2 cups vanilla ice cream
- 1/2 cup chocolate syrup
- 1/4 cup caramel sauce
- 1/2 cup chopped nuts (walnuts or almonds work well)
- 1/4 cup shredded coconut
- 1/4 cup crushed pineapple, drained
- 1/4 cup mini chocolate chips
- 1 banana, sliced
- Whipped cream for topping
- Maraschino cherries for garnish
- Optional: animal-shaped cookies for decoration

Instructions:
1. Prepare the Base:
- Scoop a generous portion of vanilla ice cream into each serving dish.
2. Drizzle with Chocolate and Caramel:
- Pour a luscious layer of chocolate syrup over the ice cream, followed by a drizzle of caramel sauce.
3. Add the Crunch:
- Sprinkle chopped nuts and shredded coconut over the top for a satisfying crunch.
4. Tropical Twist:
- Add a burst of tropical flavor with crushed pineapple, distributing it evenly among the sundaes.
5. Chocoholic's Delight:
- Sprinkle mini chocolate chips for an extra touch of chocolatey goodness.
6. Banana Bliss:
- Arrange banana slices on top, providing a creamy and fruity element to balance the sweetness.
7. Finish with Whipped Cream:
- Pile on a generous dollop of whipped cream to crown your Safari Sundae.
8. Garnish:

- Complete the adventure with a cherry on top and, if desired, decorate with animal-shaped cookies for an extra whimsical touch.

9. Serve and Enjoy:
- Dive into the Safari Sundae and experience the rich layers of flavor that transport you to the heart of Jumanji.

Nutrition Information:
(Per Serving)
- Calories: 450
- Fat: 25g
- Saturated Fat: 12g
- Cholesterol: 45mg
- Sodium: 150mg
- Carbohydrates: 55g
- Fiber: 3g
- Sugar: 40g
- Protein: 5g

Note: Nutrition information is approximate and may vary based on specific ingredients used. Adjustments can be made based on dietary preferences and restrictions. Enjoy your Safari Sundae, a cinematic treat that brings the spirit of Jumanji to your dessert table!

33. Quicksand Quiche

Embark on a culinary adventure inspired by the mystical world of Jumanji with our tantalizing "Quicksand Quiche." This savory delight is a nod to the ever-shifting landscapes and unexpected challenges encountered in the legendary game. Packed with flavorful ingredients, this quiche promises to transport your taste buds to the heart of the jungle. Are you ready to roll the dice and savor the magic of Jumanji in every bite?

Serving: 4-6 servings
Preparation Time: 15 minutes
Ready Time: 45 minutes

Ingredients:
- 1 pie crust (store-bought or homemade)

- 1 cup cooked and diced chicken
- 1 cup shredded Gruyere cheese
- 1/2 cup diced red bell pepper
- 1/2 cup diced red onion
- 1/2 cup sliced mushrooms
- 1/4 cup chopped fresh parsley
- 4 large eggs
- 1 cup milk
- 1/2 teaspoon salt
- 1/4 teaspoon black pepper
- 1/4 teaspoon paprika
- 1/4 teaspoon ground cumin

Instructions:
1. Preheat your oven to 375°F (190°C).
2. Roll out the pie crust and press it into a greased quiche or pie dish.
3. In a skillet over medium heat, sauté the diced chicken until cooked through. Remove from heat and set aside.
4. In the same skillet, add a bit of oil if needed, and sauté the red bell pepper, red onion, and mushrooms until they are tender. Mix in the cooked chicken and chopped parsley. Spread this mixture evenly over the pie crust.
5. In a bowl, whisk together the eggs, milk, salt, black pepper, paprika, and ground cumin. Pour this egg mixture over the chicken and vegetable filling in the pie crust.
6. Sprinkle the shredded Gruyere cheese on top.
7. Bake in the preheated oven for 35-40 minutes or until the quiche is set and golden brown on top.
8. Allow the quiche to cool for a few minutes before slicing and serving.

Nutrition Information:
Note: Nutritional values are approximate and may vary based on specific ingredients used.
- Calories per serving: 320
- Total Fat: 20g
- Saturated Fat: 9g
- Cholesterol: 180mg
- Sodium: 480mg
- Total Carbohydrates: 18g
- Dietary Fiber: 1g

- Sugars: 2g
- Protein: 18g

Immerse yourself in the flavors of Jumanji with this Quicksand Quiche, a dish that captures the essence of the wild and unpredictable journey. Perfect for brunch, lunch, or dinner, this quiche is sure to be a hit with adventurers and food enthusiasts alike. Enjoy the taste of Jumanji in every mouthwatering bite!

34. Vulture Vinaigrette Salad

Step into the wild and embark on a culinary adventure inspired by the heart-pounding world of Jumanji. Our "Vulture Vinaigrette Salad" pays homage to the unpredictable and thrilling nature of the game. This exotic salad combines bold flavors and textures to create a dish that will transport you to the heart of the jungle. So, tie up your boots, grab your hat, and get ready for a taste of the unexpected!

Serving: 4 servings
Preparation Time: 15 minutes
Ready Time: 20 minutes

Ingredients:
- 1 cup shredded kale
- 1 cup baby spinach
- 1 cup arugula
- 1 cup jicama, julienned
- 1 cup dragon fruit, diced
- 1/2 cup cherry tomatoes, halved
- 1/4 cup red onion, thinly sliced
- 1/4 cup toasted pumpkin seeds
- 1/4 cup crumbled feta cheese

Vulture Vinaigrette:
- 1/4 cup balsamic vinegar
- 1/3 cup extra-virgin olive oil
- 1 tablespoon honey
- 1 teaspoon Dijon mustard
- Salt and pepper to taste

Instructions:
1. Prepare the Vulture Vinaigrette:
- In a small bowl, whisk together balsamic vinegar, olive oil, honey, Dijon mustard, salt, and pepper. Set aside.
2. Assemble the Salad:
- In a large mixing bowl, combine shredded kale, baby spinach, arugula, jicama, dragon fruit, cherry tomatoes, red onion, pumpkin seeds, and feta cheese.
3. Drizzle with Vulture Vinaigrette:
- Pour the prepared Vulture Vinaigrette over the salad and toss gently to coat all ingredients evenly.
4. Serve:
- Divide the salad among four plates, ensuring each serving has a variety of ingredients.
5. Garnish (Optional):
- Garnish with additional pumpkin seeds and crumbled feta for added texture and flavor.
6. Enjoy the Adventure:
- Dive into the Vulture Vinaigrette Salad and savor the diverse flavors that mirror the excitement and unpredictability of Jumanji.

Nutrition Information:
Note: Nutrition information is approximate and may vary based on specific ingredients used.
- Calories: 250 per serving
- Protein: 5g
- Fat: 18g
- Carbohydrates: 20g
- Fiber: 5g
- Sugar: 10g
- Sodium: 200mg

Tame your taste buds and let the Vulture Vinaigrette Salad be your guide through a culinary journey inspired by the magic of Jumanji!

35. Python Pie

Embark on a culinary adventure inspired by the mystical world of Jumanji with our delightful "Python Pie." This savory pie pays homage to the jungle's inhabitants, incorporating a blend of exotic flavors and textures that will transport you into the heart of the game. Get ready to savor the wild taste of the jungle with this unique and delicious creation.

Serving: 8 servings
Preparation Time: 20 minutes
Ready Time: 1 hour 30 minutes

Ingredients:
- 1 ½ pounds python meat, diced
- 1 tablespoon olive oil
- 1 onion, finely chopped
- 2 cloves garlic, minced
- 1 cup mushrooms, sliced
- 1 cup spinach, chopped
- 1 cup potatoes, peeled and diced
- 1 cup carrots, peeled and diced
- 1 teaspoon thyme, dried
- 1 teaspoon rosemary, dried
- Salt and pepper to taste
- 1 cup chicken broth
- 1 cup heavy cream
- 1 package refrigerated pie crusts (2 crusts)

Instructions:
1. Preheat the Oven: Preheat your oven to 375°F (190°C).
2. Sauté Python Meat: In a large skillet, heat the olive oil over medium heat. Add the diced python meat and cook until browned on all sides. Remove the python meat from the skillet and set it aside.
3. Sauté Vegetables: In the same skillet, add the chopped onion and garlic. Sauté until the onion becomes translucent. Add mushrooms, spinach, potatoes, and carrots. Cook until the vegetables are tender.
4. Seasoning: Sprinkle thyme, rosemary, salt, and pepper over the vegetables. Stir to combine.
5. Combine Ingredients: Return the cooked python meat to the skillet. Pour in the chicken broth and heavy cream. Stir well to combine all the ingredients. Simmer for 10-15 minutes until the mixture thickens slightly.
6. Prepare Pie Crusts: Roll out one pie crust and line a pie dish with it. Pour the python and vegetable mixture into the pie crust. Roll out the

second pie crust and place it over the filling. Seal the edges and cut slits on the top to allow steam to escape.
7. Bake: Bake the Python Pie in the preheated oven for 40-45 minutes or until the crust is golden brown.
8. Serve: Allow the pie to cool for a few minutes before slicing. Serve warm and enjoy the wild flavors of Jumanji!

Nutrition Information:
Note: Nutritional values may vary depending on specific ingredients used.
- Calories per serving: 380
- Total Fat: 20g
- Cholesterol: 45mg
- Sodium: 450mg
- Total Carbohydrates: 30g
- Dietary Fiber: 3g
- Sugars: 2g
- Protein: 18g

Indulge in the adventurous spirit of Jumanji with this Python Pie, a culinary masterpiece that blends the untamed essence of the jungle with the comfort of a classic savory pie.

36. Viper Vermicelli

Embark on a culinary adventure inspired by the fantastical world of Jumanji with our "Viper Vermicelli" recipe. Transport yourself to the heart of the jungle with this tantalizing dish that captures the essence of excitement and danger. As you savor each bite, let the flavors unfold like the unfolding mysteries of the game itself. Get ready for a taste journey that mirrors the unpredictability of Jumanji!

Serving: 4 servings
Preparation Time: 15 minutes
Ready Time: 30 minutes

Ingredients:
- 250g vermicelli noodles
- 1 lb chicken breast, thinly sliced

- 1 cup broccoli florets
- 1 red bell pepper, thinly sliced
- 1 yellow bell pepper, thinly sliced
- 1 carrot, julienned
- 3 cloves garlic, minced
- 1 tablespoon ginger, grated
- 2 tablespoons soy sauce
- 1 tablespoon oyster sauce
- 1 tablespoon fish sauce
- 1 tablespoon hoisin sauce
- 1 tablespoon sesame oil
- 2 tablespoons vegetable oil
- 1 teaspoon chili flakes (adjust to taste)
- Fresh cilantro for garnish
- Lime wedges for serving

Instructions:
1. Cook Vermicelli: Cook the vermicelli noodles according to package instructions. Drain and set aside.
2. Prepare Sauce: In a small bowl, mix together soy sauce, oyster sauce, fish sauce, hoisin sauce, and sesame oil. Set aside.
3. Stir-fry Chicken: Heat vegetable oil in a wok or large pan over medium-high heat. Add sliced chicken and stir-fry until browned and cooked through. Remove chicken from the pan and set aside.
4. Sauté Vegetables: In the same pan, add a bit more oil if needed. Sauté garlic and ginger until fragrant. Add broccoli, bell peppers, and julienned carrots. Stir-fry until the vegetables are tender-crisp.
5. Combine and Toss: Return the cooked chicken to the pan. Add the cooked vermicelli noodles and the prepared sauce. Toss everything together until well combined and heated through.
6. Add Spice: Sprinkle chili flakes over the noodles for a hint of spice. Adjust according to your preference.
7. Garnish and Serve: Garnish with fresh cilantro and serve the Viper Vermicelli hot, accompanied by lime wedges for a burst of citrus flavor.

Nutrition Information:
(Per Serving)
- Calories: 450 kcal
- Protein: 25g
- Carbohydrates: 50g

- Fiber: 4g
- Sugars: 5g
- Fat: 18g
- Saturated Fat: 3g
- Cholesterol: 60mg
- Sodium: 800mg

Transport your taste buds to the heart of Jumanji with this Viper Vermicelli – a dish that combines the thrill of the game with the satisfaction of a delicious meal. Enjoy the journey!

37. Leopard Lemon Bars

Embark on a culinary adventure inspired by the wild and whimsical world of Jumanji with these delectable Leopard Lemon Bars. Just like the unpredictable twists and turns in the iconic film, these bars offer a delightful surprise with their zesty lemon flavor and eye-catching leopard print design. Get ready to enjoy a taste of the jungle in every bite!

Serving: Makes approximately 16 bars.
Preparation Time: 20 minutes
Ready Time: 1 hour 30 minutes (including chilling time)

Ingredients:
For the Crust:
- 1 cup all-purpose flour
- 1/2 cup unsalted butter, softened
- 1/4 cup powdered sugar
- Pinch of salt

For the Lemon Filling:
- 4 large eggs
- 1 1/2 cups granulated sugar
- 1/4 cup all-purpose flour
- 1/2 cup fresh lemon juice
- Zest of 2 lemons

For the Leopard Pattern:
- 2 tablespoons dark chocolate, melted

Instructions:

1. Preheat the oven:
- Preheat your oven to 350°F (175°C). Grease a 9x9-inch baking pan and line it with parchment paper, leaving an overhang on two opposite sides for easy removal.

2. Prepare the Crust:
- In a bowl, combine the flour, softened butter, powdered sugar, and a pinch of salt. Mix until the dough comes together.
- Press the dough evenly into the bottom of the prepared baking pan. Bake for 15-18 minutes or until lightly golden.

3. Make the Lemon Filling:
- In a separate bowl, whisk together the eggs, granulated sugar, flour, lemon juice, and lemon zest until well combined.
- Pour the lemon filling over the baked crust and return to the oven. Bake for an additional 20-25 minutes or until the edges are set, and the center is slightly jiggly.

4. Create the Leopard Pattern:
- Allow the lemon bars to cool completely in the pan. Once cooled, drizzle melted dark chocolate over the top in a random leopard print pattern.

5. Chill and Serve:
- Place the pan in the refrigerator for at least 1 hour to set the chocolate and firm up the bars. Use the parchment paper overhang to lift the bars out of the pan and onto a cutting board.
- Cut into squares and serve chilled.

Nutrition Information:
(Per serving - 1 bar)
- Calories: 180
- Total Fat: 9g
- Saturated Fat: 5g
- Cholesterol: 60mg
- Sodium: 30mg
- Total Carbohydrates: 24g
- Dietary Fiber: 1g
- Sugars: 17g
- Protein: 2g

Indulge in the magic of Jumanji with these Leopard Lemon Bars that promise to bring a burst of citrusy delight to your taste buds. The playful leopard pattern adds a touch of adventure to your dessert table, making them a perfect treat for any occasion.

38. Wild Boar Burger

Embark on a culinary adventure inspired by the untamed wilderness of Jumanji with our Wild Boar Burger recipe. Channel the spirit of the jungle as you indulge in this hearty and flavorful burger, a tribute to the thrilling world of the iconic film. This wild boar creation promises to transport your taste buds to the heart of the action, making every bite an unforgettable journey.

Serving: 4 burgers
Preparation Time: 20 minutes
Ready Time: 40 minutes

Ingredients:
- 1 pound ground wild boar meat
- 1/2 cup breadcrumbs
- 1/4 cup finely chopped red onion
- 2 cloves garlic, minced
- 1 tablespoon Worcestershire sauce
- 1 teaspoon Dijon mustard
- 1 teaspoon dried thyme
- Salt and pepper, to taste
- 4 burger buns
- 4 slices of sharp cheddar cheese
- Fresh lettuce leaves
- Sliced tomatoes
- Red onion rings
- Pickles

Instructions:
1. Prepare the Wild Boar Patties:
- In a large mixing bowl, combine the ground wild boar meat, breadcrumbs, chopped red onion, minced garlic, Worcestershire sauce, Dijon mustard, dried thyme, salt, and pepper.
- Mix the ingredients until well combined, being careful not to overwork the meat.

- Divide the mixture into four equal portions and shape them into burger patties.

2. Cook the Patties:
- Preheat a grill or grill pan over medium-high heat.
- Cook the wild boar patties for about 4-5 minutes per side, or until they reach your desired level of doneness.
- During the last minute of cooking, place a slice of cheddar cheese on each patty and allow it to melt.

3. Assemble the Burgers:
- Toast the burger buns on the grill for a minute or until they are golden brown.
- Place a wild boar patty with melted cheddar on the bottom half of each bun.
- Top with fresh lettuce leaves, sliced tomatoes, red onion rings, and pickles.
- Place the other half of the bun on top.

4. Serve:
- Plate the Wild Boar Burgers and serve them hot, accompanied by your favorite side dishes or a side of crispy fries.

Nutrition Information:
Note: Nutrition information is approximate and may vary based on specific ingredients used.
- Calories per serving: XXX
- Total Fat: XXg
- Saturated Fat: XXg
- Cholesterol: XXmg
- Sodium: XXXmg
- Total Carbohydrates: XXg
- Dietary Fiber: XXg
- Sugars: XXg
- Protein: XXg

Indulge in the essence of Jumanji with this Wild Boar Burger, a culinary tribute to the adventurous and unpredictable spirit of the film. Each bite is a journey into the untamed flavors of the wild, making this burger a perfect addition to your movie-inspired feast.

39. Tarantula Tacos

Embark on a culinary adventure inspired by the wild world of Jumanji with these Tarantula Tacos! Channeling the daring spirit of the jungle, these tacos pay homage to the movie's unpredictable and exciting twists. Don't worry, no actual tarantulas were harmed in the making of these tacos; instead, we use crispy and flavorful ingredients to capture the essence of the jungle in each bite.

Serving: Makes 4 servings.
Preparation Time: 20 minutes
Ready Time: 35 minutes

Ingredients:
- 8 small corn tortillas
- 2 cups shredded lettuce
- 1 cup diced tomatoes
- 1 cup shredded cheddar cheese
- 1 cup sour cream
- 1 lime, cut into wedges
- Fresh cilantro, chopped, for garnish

Tarantula Filling:
- 2 cups shredded cooked chicken (or substitute with black beans for a vegetarian option)
- 1 teaspoon chili powder
- 1 teaspoon cumin
- 1/2 teaspoon garlic powder
- Salt and pepper to taste

Crispy Tarantula Legs:
- 16 long pretzel sticks
- 1 cup panko breadcrumbs
- 1/2 cup all-purpose flour
- 2 large eggs, beaten
- Cooking spray

Instructions:
1. Preheat your oven to 375°F (190°C).
2. In a bowl, mix the shredded chicken (or black beans) with chili powder, cumin, garlic powder, salt, and pepper. Set aside.

3. For the crispy tarantula legs, dip each pretzel stick into flour, then beaten eggs, and finally coat with panko breadcrumbs. Place them on a baking sheet and lightly spray with cooking spray. Bake for 10-12 minutes or until golden brown and crispy.
4. Warm the corn tortillas in a dry skillet or microwave.
5. Assemble the tacos by placing a generous amount of the seasoned chicken (or black beans) on each tortilla.
6. Top with shredded lettuce, diced tomatoes, cheddar cheese, and a dollop of sour cream.
7. Garnish with fresh cilantro and serve with lime wedges on the side.
8. Add the crispy tarantula legs on top for a crunchy and adventurous twist.

Nutrition Information:
(Per Serving)
- Calories: 450
- Protein: 25g
- Fat: 20g
- Carbohydrates: 45g
- Fiber: 6g
- Sugar: 3g
- Sodium: 600mg

Embrace the unexpected with these Tarantula Tacos, a nod to the Jumanji universe that will have your taste buds swinging from vine to vine in delight!

40. Hyena Hash

In the adventurous world of Jumanji, unexpected encounters and thrilling escapades await at every turn. Inspired by this unpredictable journey, Hyena Hash captures the essence of excitement and surprise. This hearty dish combines a medley of flavors and textures, making it a culinary adventure on its own. Just like the game, this dish promises an exhilarating experience for your taste buds.

Serving: 4 servings
Preparation time: 15 minutes
Ready time: 40 minutes

Ingredients:
- 4 medium potatoes, diced
- 1 pound ground beef
- 1 onion, finely chopped
- 2 cloves garlic, minced
- 1 red bell pepper, diced
- 1 green bell pepper, diced
- 1 can (14 ounces) diced tomatoes
- 1 teaspoon paprika
- 1 teaspoon cumin
- Salt and pepper to taste
- 4 eggs
- Chopped fresh parsley for garnish

Instructions:
1. Prepare the Potatoes: Parboil the diced potatoes in a pot of salted water for about 5 minutes. Drain and set aside.
2. Cook the Beef: In a large skillet over medium heat, brown the ground beef. Once cooked through, remove it from the skillet and set it aside.
3. Saute Aromatics: In the same skillet, add a little oil if needed and sauté the onion and garlic until translucent.
4. Add Peppers and Potatoes: Stir in the diced red and green bell peppers along with the parboiled diced potatoes. Cook for about 5 minutes until the potatoes start to turn golden.
5. Season and Simmer: Add the browned beef back into the skillet. Stir in the diced tomatoes, paprika, cumin, salt, and pepper. Allow the mixture to simmer for 10-15 minutes, ensuring the flavors meld together.
6. Make Wells for Eggs: Create four wells in the hash mixture with the back of a spoon. Crack an egg into each well. Cover the skillet and cook for about 5-7 minutes, or until the eggs reach your desired level of doneness.
7. Garnish and Serve: Sprinkle chopped fresh parsley over the Hyena Hash before serving.

Nutrition Information (per serving):
- Calories: 420 kcal
- Total Fat: 20g
- Saturated Fat: 7g
- Cholesterol: 220mg

- Sodium: 460mg
- Total Carbohydrates: 32g
- Dietary Fiber: 5g
- Sugars: 6g
- Protein: 29g

This Hyena Hash is a vibrant and flavorsome dish that celebrates the unpredictable nature of Jumanji. Enjoy the thrill of every bite as you embark on your own culinary adventure!

41. Rhino Ramen

In the unpredictable realm of Jumanji, where adventure and surprises await at every turn, comes the hearty and flavorful Rhino Ramen. Inspired by the resilience of the rhinoceros and the boldness of the Jumanji jungle, this dish combines robust flavors and comforting warmth to fuel your journey through any challenge.

Serving: Serves: 4
Preparation Time: 15 minutes
Ready Time: Total: 45 minutes

Ingredients:
- 8 cups chicken or vegetable broth
- 300g ramen noodles
- 1 tablespoon sesame oil
- 1 tablespoon vegetable oil
- 1 onion, finely chopped
- 3 cloves garlic, minced
- 1-inch piece of ginger, grated
- 1 red bell pepper, thinly sliced
- 200g shiitake mushrooms, sliced
- 2 cups baby spinach
- 1 tablespoon soy sauce
- 1 tablespoon rice vinegar
- Salt and pepper to taste
- Optional toppings: sliced green onions, soft-boiled eggs, chili oil

Instructions:

1. Prepare Broth: In a large pot, bring the chicken or vegetable broth to a gentle simmer over medium heat.
2. Cook Noodles: Cook the ramen noodles according to package instructions in a separate pot. Drain and set aside.
3. Sauté Aromatics: In a large skillet or wok, heat sesame and vegetable oil over medium heat. Sauté the chopped onion, garlic, and ginger until fragrant and lightly golden.
4. Add Vegetables: Add the sliced red bell pepper and shiitake mushrooms to the skillet. Stir-fry for a few minutes until the vegetables start to soften.
5. Combine Ingredients: Pour the sautéed vegetables into the pot with the simmering broth. Add the baby spinach, soy sauce, and rice vinegar. Allow the flavors to meld together for about 5-7 minutes.
6. Season and Serve: Season the broth with salt and pepper to taste. Divide the cooked ramen noodles into serving bowls. Ladle the flavorful broth and vegetables over the noodles.
7. Garnish: Garnish with sliced green onions, a drizzle of chili oil, and if desired, a soft-boiled egg.

Nutrition Information (per serving):
- Calories: 350
- Protein: 12g
- Carbohydrates: 50g
- Fat: 12g
- Fiber: 5g
- Sodium: 1200mg

Enjoy the robust flavors and comforting warmth of Rhino Ramen, a dish inspired by the untamed adventures of Jumanji!

42. Jumanji Jerky

Embark on a flavorful journey through the wilds of Jumanji with this tantalizing Jumanji Jerky recipe. Inspired by the adventure-packed film, this jerky promises a blend of spices that'll transport your taste buds to uncharted territories.

Serving: Makes about 8 servings
Preparation Time: 15 minutes (plus marinating time)

Ready Time: 8-10 hours

Ingredients:
- 2 pounds beef (flank steak or top round), thinly sliced against the grain
- 1/2 cup soy sauce
- 1/4 cup Worcestershire sauce
- 2 tablespoons brown sugar
- 1 tablespoon smoked paprika
- 1 teaspoon onion powder
- 1 teaspoon garlic powder
- 1 teaspoon black pepper
- 1/2 teaspoon cayenne pepper (adjust for desired heat)
- 1/2 teaspoon ground cumin
- 1/4 teaspoon cinnamon
- Cooking spray or oil for greasing

Instructions:
1. In a mixing bowl, combine the soy sauce, Worcestershire sauce, brown sugar, smoked paprika, onion powder, garlic powder, black pepper, cayenne pepper, cumin, and cinnamon. Stir until the sugar is dissolved.
2. Place the thinly sliced beef into a resealable plastic bag or a shallow dish. Pour the marinade over the beef, ensuring all pieces are coated. Seal the bag or cover the dish and refrigerate for at least 4 hours, or ideally overnight, to allow the flavors to meld.
3. Preheat your oven to 175°F (80°C) or the lowest setting.
4. Remove the marinated beef from the refrigerator and let it come to room temperature for about 30 minutes.
5. Place a wire rack on top of a baking sheet and lightly grease the rack with cooking spray or oil.
6. Arrange the marinated beef slices in a single layer on the prepared wire rack.
7. Place the baking sheet in the preheated oven and bake the beef for 4-6 hours, or until the jerky is dried and firm, but still pliable. Rotate the baking sheet halfway through the cooking time for even drying.
8. Once done, remove the jerky from the oven and let it cool completely on the wire rack. Blot any excess oil with paper towels, if needed.
9. Store the Jumanji Jerky in an airtight container or resealable bags at room temperature for up to 2 weeks. Enjoy your flavorful adventure snack!

Nutrition Information (per serving):
Note: Nutritional values may vary based on ingredients used and portion sizes.
- Calories: Approximately 180
- Protein: Approximately 20g
- Fat: Approximately 8g
- Carbohydrates: Approximately 5g
- Fiber: Approximately 0.5g

This Jumanji Jerky is a savory and protein-packed snack that's perfect for fueling your adventures or enjoying a taste of the wild while watching the film.

43. Crocodile Ceviche

Embark on a culinary adventure inspired by the wild and untamed spirit of Jumanji with this exotic twist on a classic dish - Crocodile Ceviche. Transport yourself to the heart of the jungle as you savor the flavors of succulent crocodile meat paired with zesty citrus and vibrant herbs. This dish captures the essence of the untamed wilderness and the thrill of the game. Get ready to experience the unexpected with every bite!

Serving: 4 servings
Preparation Time: 20 minutes
Ready Time: 2 hours (including marination time)

Ingredients:
- 1 pound fresh crocodile meat, diced
- 1 cup lime juice (about 8-10 limes)
- 1 cup lemon juice (about 4-6 lemons)
- 1 red onion, finely chopped
- 1 bell pepper (red or yellow), diced
- 1 cucumber, peeled and diced
- 2 tomatoes, seeded and chopped
- 1/2 cup fresh cilantro, chopped
- 1 jalapeño, seeded and finely chopped
- Salt and pepper to taste
- 2 tablespoons olive oil
- Tortilla chips or plantain chips for serving

Instructions:
1. Prepare the Crocodile Meat:
- Ensure the crocodile meat is fresh and clean.
- Dice the meat into small, bite-sized pieces.
2. Citrus Marinade:
- In a large bowl, combine the lime juice, lemon juice, and olive oil.
- Place the diced crocodile meat into the citrus marinade, ensuring each piece is coated.
- Cover the bowl and refrigerate for at least 2 hours, allowing the citrus to "cook" the crocodile meat.
3. Combine the Ingredients:
- After marination, drain excess citrus marinade.
- In a separate bowl, combine the marinated crocodile meat with chopped red onion, bell pepper, cucumber, tomatoes, cilantro, and jalapeño.
- Gently mix the ingredients, ensuring an even distribution.
4. Season and Chill:
- Season the ceviche with salt and pepper according to taste.
- Cover the bowl and refrigerate for an additional 30 minutes to let the flavors meld.
5. Serve:
- Spoon the crocodile ceviche into individual serving bowls.
- Garnish with extra cilantro and a slice of lime.
- Serve with tortilla chips or plantain chips on the side.

Nutrition Information:
(Per Serving)
- Calories: 250
- Protein: 25g
- Carbohydrates: 15g
- Fat: 10g
- Fiber: 3g
- Sugar: 5g
- Sodium: 400mg

Dive into the world of Jumanji with this Crocodile Ceviche – a dish that tantalizes the taste buds and transports you to the heart of the jungle. Enjoy the thrill of the game both on the screen and on your plate!

44. Bamboo Shoot Smoothie

Embark on a culinary adventure inspired by the enchanting world of Jumanji with our Bamboo Shoot Smoothie. Just like the movie's lush and mysterious jungle, this smoothie promises a delightful blend of flavors that will transport your taste buds to a tropical paradise. Packed with the goodness of bamboo shoots, this smoothie is a unique and refreshing treat that will leave you craving more.

Serving: 2 servings
Preparation Time: 15 minutes
Ready Time: 20 minutes

Ingredients:
- 1 cup bamboo shoots, cooked and sliced
- 1 banana, peeled and sliced
- 1/2 cup pineapple chunks
- 1/2 cup coconut milk
- 1/2 cup Greek yogurt
- 1 tablespoon honey
- 1/2 teaspoon ginger, grated
- 1/2 teaspoon turmeric powder
- 1 cup ice cubes

Instructions:
1. Prepare Bamboo Shoots: If using fresh bamboo shoots, boil them until tender and slice them into thin strips.
2. Blend Ingredients: In a blender, combine the bamboo shoots, banana, pineapple chunks, coconut milk, Greek yogurt, honey, grated ginger, turmeric powder, and ice cubes.
3. Blend Until Smooth: Blend the ingredients until smooth and creamy, ensuring all the ingredients are well incorporated.
4. Adjust Consistency: If the smoothie is too thick, you can add more coconut milk or water to reach your desired consistency.
5. Serve: Pour the bamboo shoot smoothie into glasses and garnish with a pineapple wedge or a bamboo shoot slice for an extra touch of presentation.
6. Enjoy: Sip and savor the unique flavors inspired by the Jumanji universe. Let the tropical essence of bamboo shoots transport you to the heart of the jungle.

Nutrition Information:
(Per Serving)
- Calories: 220
- Protein: 8g
- Fat: 6g
- Carbohydrates: 38g
- Fiber: 4g
- Sugar: 24g
- Vitamin C: 45mg
- Calcium: 120mg
- Iron: 2mg

Indulge in the magic of Jumanji with this Bamboo Shoot Smoothie – a cinematic experience for your taste buds!

45. Python Popcorn

Embark on a wild and flavorful journey with our "Python Popcorn," inspired by the thrilling world of Jumanji. This unique popcorn recipe captures the essence of adventure and excitement, making it the perfect snack to enjoy while immersing yourself in the magic of the Jumanji universe.

Serving: Ideal for sharing among 4-6 hungry adventurers.
Preparation Time: 15 minutes
Ready Time: 20 minutes

Ingredients:
- 1/2 cup popcorn kernels
- 3 tablespoons vegetable oil
- 1/4 cup unsalted butter
- 1 cup green and yellow candy melts
- 1 cup pretzel sticks, broken into pieces
- 1/2 cup gummy snakes (Python-inspired)
- 1/4 cup chocolate-covered insects (optional for the brave)
- Salt to taste

Instructions:

1. Pop the Corn:
- In a large, heavy-bottomed pot, heat the vegetable oil over medium heat.
- Add the popcorn kernels, cover with a lid, and shake the pot occasionally until the popping slows down.
- Remove from heat and let any remaining kernels pop with the residual heat.
- Transfer the popcorn to a large bowl, removing any unpopped kernels.

2. Prepare the Python Coating:
- In a microwave-safe bowl, melt the butter and candy melts in 30-second intervals, stirring between each, until smooth.

3. Coat the Popcorn:
- Drizzle the melted candy over the popcorn, tossing gently to coat evenly.
- Add a pinch of salt to enhance the flavor.

4. Add the Crunch:
- Mix in the pretzel pieces, ensuring they are evenly distributed throughout the popcorn.

5. Introduce the Python:
- Carefully place the gummy snakes on top of the popcorn, creating a playful and adventurous appearance.

6. Optional Insect Encounter:
- For the truly daring, sprinkle chocolate-covered insects over the popcorn for an extra layer of excitement.

7. Let It Set:
- Allow the popcorn to cool and the coating to set for about 10 minutes.

8. Serve and Enjoy:
- Gently break apart any clumps and serve this Python Popcorn creation to your fellow explorers as you dive into the Jumanji-themed feast.

Nutrition Information:
(Per serving, based on 6 servings)
- Calories: 320
- Total Fat: 18g
- Saturated Fat: 9g
- Trans Fat: 0g
- Cholesterol: 20mg
- Sodium: 300mg
- Total Carbohydrates: 40g
- Dietary Fiber: 3g

- Sugars: 20g
- Protein: 3g

Dive into the untamed world of Jumanji with this Python Popcorn recipe, a perfect blend of sweet, savory, and adventurous flavors. Grab your popcorn bowl and get ready for a cinematic snacking experience!

46. Cobra Crepes

Step into the wild and adventurous world of Jumanji with these exotic and thrilling Cobra Crepes. Inspired by the mysterious and vibrant landscapes of the film, these crepes are not only a feast for the taste buds but also a visual delight. Packed with bold flavors and a touch of danger, these crepes are perfect for those who crave excitement in every bite.

Serving: Makes 4 servings
Preparation Time: 15 minutes
Ready Time: 30 minutes

Ingredients:
- 1 cup all-purpose flour
- 2 eggs
- 1/2 cup milk
- 1/2 cup water
- 1/4 teaspoon salt
- 2 tablespoons melted butter
- 1 tablespoon cocoa powder
- 1 tablespoon sugar
- Cooking spray or additional butter for greasing the pan

For the Filling:
- 1 cup sliced strawberries
- 1/2 cup whipped cream
- 1/4 cup chocolate chips
- 4 gummy snakes (edible)

Instructions:
1. In a blender, combine the flour, eggs, milk, water, salt, melted butter, cocoa powder, and sugar. Blend until the batter is smooth and well combined.

2. Heat a non-stick crepe pan or skillet over medium heat. Lightly grease the pan with cooking spray or butter.
3. Pour 1/4 cup of the batter into the center of the pan, swirling it around to spread evenly. Cook for about 1-2 minutes or until the edges start to lift. Flip the crepe and cook for an additional 1-2 minutes on the other side. Repeat with the remaining batter.
4. Once all the crepes are cooked, lay them out on a flat surface.
5. To assemble, spread a layer of whipped cream on each crepe, add sliced strawberries, and sprinkle with chocolate chips. Roll the crepes and arrange them on a serving plate.
6. Place a gummy snake on top of each rolled crepe for that adventurous touch.
7. Serve the Cobra Crepes immediately and savor the wild flavors inspired by Jumanji.

Nutrition Information:
(Per serving)
- Calories: 280
- Total Fat: 12g
- Saturated Fat: 7g
- Cholesterol: 110mg
- Sodium: 220mg
- Total Carbohydrates: 36g
- Dietary Fiber: 2g
- Sugars: 12g
- Protein: 7g

Indulge in the magic of Jumanji with these Cobra Crepes, where every bite is an escapade into the unknown.

47. Monkey Mango Sorbet

Embark on a wild culinary adventure inspired by the heart-pounding jungle escapades of Jumanji with our delightful Monkey Mango Sorbet. This frozen treat captures the essence of the tropical paradise within the iconic game, blending the sweetness of ripe mangoes with a playful touch of mischief. Let the flavors transport you to a world where every bite is an invitation to join the lively spirit of Jumanji.

Serving: Serves 4
Preparation Time: 15 minutes
Ready Time: 4 hours (including freezing time)

Ingredients:
- 3 large ripe mangoes, peeled, pitted, and diced
- 1/2 cup coconut milk
- 1/3 cup honey or maple syrup
- 1 tablespoon fresh lime juice
- 1 teaspoon vanilla extract
- Pinch of salt
- 1/4 cup shredded coconut, toasted (for garnish)
- Sliced bananas and mint leaves (optional, for garnish)

Instructions:
1. In a blender, combine the diced mangoes, coconut milk, honey (or maple syrup), lime juice, vanilla extract, and a pinch of salt. Blend until smooth and creamy.
2. Taste the mixture and adjust sweetness or acidity if needed by adding more honey or lime juice.
3. Pour the sorbet mixture into an ice cream maker and churn according to the manufacturer's instructions until it reaches a thick, sorbet-like consistency.
4. Transfer the sorbet to a lidded container, smoothing the top with a spatula. Cover and freeze for at least 4 hours or until firm.
5. Before serving, toast the shredded coconut in a dry pan over medium heat until golden brown. Let it cool.
6. Scoop the Monkey Mango Sorbet into bowls or cones. Garnish with toasted shredded coconut and, if desired, add a slice of banana and a sprig of mint for an extra touch of jungle freshness.

Nutrition Information:
(Per Serving)
- Calories: 180
- Total Fat: 5g
- Saturated Fat: 4g
- Cholesterol: 0mg
- Sodium: 30mg
- Total Carbohydrates: 38g
- Dietary Fiber: 3g

- Sugars: 33g
- Protein: 1g

Indulge in the flavors of Jumanji with this Monkey Mango Sorbet, a tantalizing treat that brings the excitement of the game to your taste buds. Perfect for cooling off during the heat of the jungle or impressing guests at your next movie night.

48. Leopard Latte

Transport yourself to the heart of the Jumanji jungle with this exotic and visually stunning beverage inspired by the enchanting world of the film. The Leopard Latte is a delightful blend of rich espresso and creamy frothed milk, adorned with a mesmerizing leopard print pattern that mirrors the mysterious and thrilling essence of Jumanji. Immerse yourself in the magic of the jungle as you sip on this delicious concoction, making every moment an adventure.

Serving: 1 serving
Preparation Time: 15 minutes
Ready Time: 20 minutes

Ingredients:
- 1 shot of espresso
- 1 cup of milk (dairy or plant-based)
- 1 tablespoon of cocoa powder
- 1 tablespoon of honey or sweetener of choice
- 1/2 teaspoon of vanilla extract
- Pinch of cinnamon
- Pinch of salt

Instructions:
1. Brew the Espresso:
Start by brewing a shot of espresso using your preferred method.
2. Froth the Milk:
Heat the milk in a saucepan or using a milk frother until it's warm and frothy.
3. Create the Leopard Print:

In a small bowl, mix the cocoa powder, honey, vanilla extract, cinnamon, and a pinch of salt to create a smooth paste.
4. Assemble the Leopard Latte:
Pour the frothed milk over the espresso, holding back the foam with a spoon. Spoon the cocoa paste onto the foam, creating irregular spots resembling a leopard print.
5. Swirl and Enjoy:
Use a toothpick or a thin skewer to swirl the cocoa paste into a leopard print pattern on the surface of the latte.
6. Garnish (Optional):
Optionally, sprinkle a bit of extra cocoa powder or cinnamon on top for an extra touch of flavor and aesthetics.
7. Serve and Indulge:
Your Leopard Latte is now ready to be served. Enjoy the rich flavors and intricate design inspired by the wild adventures of Jumanji.

Nutrition Information:
Note: Nutrition information may vary based on the type of milk and sweetener used.
- Calories: Approximately 120 kcal
- Protein: 6g
- Fat: 5g
- Carbohydrates: 15g
- Fiber: 1g
- Sugar: 12g
- Calcium: 200mg
- Iron: 1mg

Transport yourself into the heart of the Jumanji jungle with each sip of this Leopard Latte, a perfect blend of adventure and indulgence.

49. Jungle Jello

Step into the mystical world of Jumanji with a delightful treat that mirrors the jungle's vibrant and exotic essence – Jungle Jello! This playful dessert, inspired by the film Jumanji, combines the thrill of the game with the joy of indulging in a tantalizing and visually stunning treat. Embark on a culinary adventure as you create this whimsical dessert that captures the spirit of the wild. Get ready to savor the taste of the jungle in every delicious bite!

Serving: 8 servings
Preparation Time: 20 minutes
Ready Time: 4 hours (including chilling time)

Ingredients:
- 2 packages (6 oz each) of green lime-flavored gelatin
- 2 cups boiling water
- 1 cup cold water
- 1 cup pineapple juice
- 1 can (20 oz) crushed pineapple, drained
- 1 cup coconut milk
- 1/2 cup sweetened condensed milk
- Assorted gummy animals (for garnish)
- Fresh mint leaves (for garnish)

Instructions:
1. In a large mixing bowl, combine the two packages of green lime-flavored gelatin. Pour in the boiling water and stir until the gelatin is completely dissolved.
2. Add the cold water and pineapple juice to the gelatin mixture, stirring well to combine.
3. Allow the gelatin mixture to cool to room temperature. Once cooled, refrigerate for about 30 minutes to slightly set the gelatin.
4. Remove the bowl from the refrigerator and gently fold in the drained crushed pineapple.
5. In a separate bowl, whisk together the coconut milk and sweetened condensed milk until well combined.
6. Carefully pour the coconut milk mixture over the partially set gelatin mixture, creating a second layer. Use a spoon to spread the mixture evenly.
7. Return the bowl to the refrigerator and let it chill for at least 4 hours or until fully set.
8. Once the Jungle Jello is set, cut it into squares or use jungle-themed cookie cutters for a playful touch.
9. Garnish each serving with assorted gummy animals and fresh mint leaves to enhance the jungle theme.

10. Serve chilled and watch as your guests embark on their own Jumanji-inspired culinary adventure!

Nutrition Information:
(Per serving)
- Calories: 180
- Total Fat: 4g
- Saturated Fat: 3g
- Cholesterol: 7mg
- Sodium: 56mg
- Total Carbohydrates: 34g
- Dietary Fiber: 1g
- Sugars: 28g
- Protein: 3g

Note: Nutrition information is approximate and may vary based on specific ingredients and serving sizes.

50. Watermelon Waterfall

Embark on a culinary adventure inspired by the wild and magical world of Jumanji with our refreshing concoction, the "Watermelon Waterfall." Just like the unexpected twists and turns in the game, this drink will take your taste buds on a thrilling journey of flavors. Dive into the essence of the jungle with this vibrant and hydrating beverage that pays homage to the lush landscapes encountered in the film.

Serving: Serves 4
Preparation Time: 15 minutes
Ready Time: 1 hour (including chilling time)

Ingredients:
- 1 small seedless watermelon, chilled and cubed
- 1 cup fresh blueberries
- 1 lime, juiced
- 2 tablespoons honey or agave syrup
- 1 cup coconut water
- Ice cubes
- Mint leaves for garnish

Instructions:
1. Prepare the Watermelon:
- Cut the watermelon into small cubes, discarding any seeds.
- Place the watermelon cubes in a blender.
2. Blend the Watermelon:
- Blend the watermelon until smooth and liquid.
- Strain the watermelon juice to remove any pulp.
3. Mix in Blueberries:
- In a pitcher, combine the watermelon juice with fresh blueberries.
4. Add Lime and Sweetener:
- Squeeze the juice of one lime into the mixture.
- Add honey or agave syrup for sweetness.
5. Incorporate Coconut Water:
- Pour in the coconut water and stir the mixture gently.
6. Chill the Mixture:
- Place the pitcher in the refrigerator and let the flavors meld for at least an hour.
7. Serve:
- Fill glasses with ice cubes.
- Pour the chilled Watermelon Waterfall mixture into the glasses.
8. Garnish and Enjoy:
- Garnish each glass with a sprig of mint.
- Stir gently before sipping to experience the full blend of flavors.

Nutrition Information (per serving):
- Calories: 90
- Total Fat: 0g
- Cholesterol: 0mg
- Sodium: 25mg
- Total Carbohydrates: 22g
- Dietary Fiber: 2g
- Sugars: 17g
- Protein: 1g

Embrace the spirit of Jumanji with the Watermelon Waterfall, a drink that mirrors the excitement and unpredictability of the jungle. Refreshing and delicious, this beverage is perfect for cooling down after a thrilling adventure or simply enjoying the magic of cinema-inspired cuisine.

51. Baboon Banana Smoothie

Embark on a wild culinary adventure inspired by the untamed spirit of Jumanji with our Baboon Banana Smoothie. Crafted to capture the essence of the jungle, this smoothie pays homage to the mischievous baboons that bring an element of surprise to the magical world of Jumanji. Brace yourself for a flavorful journey that mirrors the excitement of the game itself.

Serving: 2 servings
Preparation Time: 10 minutes
Ready Time: 10 minutes

Ingredients:
- 2 ripe bananas, peeled and sliced
- 1 cup frozen mixed berries (strawberries, blueberries, raspberries)
- 1/2 cup Greek yogurt
- 1 tablespoon honey
- 1 cup coconut water
- 1/2 cup orange juice
- 1/2 teaspoon vanilla extract
- 1 cup ice cubes
- Optional: banana slices and mint leaves for garnish

Instructions:
1. In a blender, combine the sliced bananas, frozen mixed berries, Greek yogurt, honey, coconut water, orange juice, vanilla extract, and ice cubes.
2. Blend on high speed until the mixture is smooth and creamy.
3. Pause and scrape down the sides of the blender if needed to ensure all ingredients are well incorporated.
4. Taste the smoothie and adjust sweetness or thickness as desired by adding more honey or liquid.
5. Once satisfied with the consistency, pour the smoothie into glasses.
6. Optional: Garnish with banana slices and a sprig of fresh mint for a decorative touch.
7. Serve immediately and enjoy the tropical flavors of the Baboon Banana Smoothie!

Nutrition Information:

Note: Nutrition values are approximate and may vary based on specific ingredients and quantities used.
- Calories per serving: 180
- Total Fat: 1g
- Saturated Fat: 0.5g
- Cholesterol: 2mg
- Sodium: 45mg
- Total Carbohydrates: 42g
- Dietary Fiber: 5g
- Sugars: 27g
- Protein: 4g

Sip on this vibrant smoothie as you immerse yourself in the spirit of Jumanji, and let the Baboon Banana Smoothie transport you to the heart of the jungle with every delicious sip.

52. Elephant Eye Eggs

Embark on a culinary adventure inspired by the wild and whimsical world of Jumanji with our unique recipe for "Elephant Eye Eggs." In the spirit of the mysterious and fantastical, these eggs offer a delightful twist to your breakfast or brunch table. The name pays homage to the incredible creatures encountered in the Jumanji film, and the taste is just as adventurous as the game itself.

Serving: 4 servings
Preparation Time: 15 minutes
Ready Time: 25 minutes

Ingredients:
- 4 large eggs
- 2 avocados, ripe
- 1 tablespoon olive oil
- 1 teaspoon lime juice
- Salt and pepper to taste
- 1 tablespoon chopped fresh cilantro
- 1 tablespoon diced red bell pepper
- 1 tablespoon diced red onion
- Hot sauce (optional, for spice lovers)

Instructions:
1. Preheat the Oven: Preheat your oven to 375°F (190°C).
2. Prepare the Avocado Mix: In a bowl, mash the ripe avocados. Add olive oil, lime juice, salt, and pepper. Mix well until you achieve a smooth consistency.
3. Prepare the Eggs: Carefully crack each egg into a small bowl to ensure no shell pieces make it into the final dish.
4. Make Elephant Eye Nests: In a baking dish, create four small nests using the avocado mixture. Spoon the mixture onto the dish, leaving a well in the center for the eggs.
5. Add the Eggs: Gently pour one egg into each avocado nest.
6. Season and Bake: Sprinkle the eggs with salt and pepper. Bake in the preheated oven for 15-18 minutes or until the egg whites are set, but the yolks are still runny.
7. Garnish: Remove from the oven and sprinkle chopped cilantro, diced red bell pepper, and red onion over the eggs.
8. Serve: Optionally, add a dash of hot sauce for an extra kick. Serve the Elephant Eye Eggs warm, and enjoy the adventure on your plate!

Nutrition Information:
(Per Serving)
- Calories: 250
- Total Fat: 20g
- Saturated Fat: 4g
- Trans Fat: 0g
- Cholesterol: 185mg
- Sodium: 120mg
- Total Carbohydrates: 10g
- Dietary Fiber: 7g
- Sugars: 1g
- Protein: 10g

Note: Nutrition values are approximate and may vary based on specific ingredients used. Adjust quantities to meet your dietary preferences and restrictions.

53. Ostrich Oreo Cake

Embark on a wild culinary adventure inspired by the untamed world of Jumanji with our Ostrich Oreo Cake. This delectable dessert pays homage to the exotic and unpredictable nature of the Jumanji film series. The combination of rich ostrich meat and the irresistible crunch of Oreo cookies creates a unique and unforgettable flavor experience that will transport you straight into the heart of the jungle. Get ready to indulge in a taste sensation like no other!

Serving: Serves 8-10
Preparation Time: 20 minutes
Ready Time: 1 hour 30 minutes

Ingredients:
- 1 pound ostrich meat, ground
- 1 cup crushed Oreo cookies (about 10 cookies for the batter, and 5 for topping)
- 1 cup all-purpose flour
- 1 cup granulated sugar
- 1/2 cup unsweetened cocoa powder
- 1 teaspoon baking powder
- 1/2 teaspoon baking soda
- 1/2 teaspoon salt
- 1 cup buttermilk
- 1/2 cup vegetable oil
- 2 large eggs
- 1 teaspoon vanilla extract
- 1 cup boiling water

Instructions:
1. Preheat your oven to 350°F (175°C). Grease and flour two 9-inch round cake pans.
2. In a large bowl, combine the ground ostrich meat, crushed Oreo cookies, flour, sugar, cocoa powder, baking powder, baking soda, and salt. Mix until well combined.
3. In a separate bowl, whisk together the buttermilk, vegetable oil, eggs, and vanilla extract.
4. Gradually add the wet ingredients to the dry ingredients, mixing well after each addition.
5. Stir in the boiling water until the batter is smooth. The batter will be thin, but that's normal.

6. Pour the batter evenly into the prepared cake pans.
7. Bake in the preheated oven for 30 to 35 minutes, or until a toothpick inserted into the center comes out clean.
8. Allow the cakes to cool in the pans for 10 minutes before transferring them to a wire rack to cool completely.
9. Once the cakes are cool, spread a layer of your favorite frosting between them and on top.
10. Crush the remaining 5 Oreo cookies and sprinkle the crumbs over the frosted cake for a delightful and crunchy topping.

Nutrition Information:
Note: Nutrition information is approximate and may vary based on specific ingredients used.
- Calories: 420 per serving
- Fat: 18g
- Cholesterol: 45mg
- Sodium: 380mg
- Carbohydrates: 56g
- Fiber: 3g
- Sugar: 36g
- Protein: 9g

Indulge in the Jumanji experience with this Ostrich Oreo Cake – a tantalizing combination of flavors that will leave your taste buds in awe. Enjoy the journey into the wild side of culinary exploration!

54. Rockslide Rock Candy

Embark on a culinary adventure inspired by the thrilling world of Jumanji with our "Rockslide Rock Candy." This sweet treat pays homage to the movie's unpredictable and exciting landscapes, capturing the essence of the wild and mysterious journey. Brace yourself for a flavorful ride as you create these crystalline delights reminiscent of the perilous rockslide scenes in Jumanji.

Serving: Makes approximately 12 servings.
Preparation Time: 15 minutes.
Ready Time: 3-4 hours (including cooling time).

Ingredients:
- 2 cups granulated sugar
- 1/2 cup water
- 1/2 cup light corn syrup
- 1/2 teaspoon cream of tartar
- 1 teaspoon flavored extract (such as raspberry or cherry)
- Assorted edible rock candy or crushed hard candies
- Optional: Food coloring

Instructions:
1. Prepare the Candy Mixture:
- In a medium saucepan, combine sugar, water, corn syrup, and cream of tartar over medium heat. Stir until the sugar dissolves.
2. Cook the Mixture:
- Bring the mixture to a boil without stirring. Use a candy thermometer and cook until it reaches the hard-crack stage (300°F or 150°C). This usually takes about 10-15 minutes.
3. Flavor and Color:
- Remove the mixture from heat and let it cool for a couple of minutes. Stir in the flavored extract of your choice. Add food coloring if desired.
4. Prepare the Surface:
- Line a baking sheet with parchment paper. If you're using rock-shaped molds, lightly grease them.
5. Pour the Candy:
- Carefully pour the hot candy mixture onto the prepared surface or into molds. Allow it to spread naturally or use a spatula to shape it if needed.
6. Add Rock Candy:
- While the candy is still hot and pliable, press edible rock candy or crushed hard candies into the surface to create a rocky texture. Be creative and mimic the rugged terrain of Jumanji.
7. Cool and Break:
- Let the candy cool and harden completely, which usually takes about 2-3 hours. Once hardened, break it into pieces resembling rock formations.
8. Serve:
- Arrange the Rockslide Rock Candy pieces on a serving platter and relish the adventure-inspired sweet delight.

Nutrition Information:
Note: Nutrition information may vary based on specific ingredients used and serving sizes.

- Serving Size: 1 piece
- Calories: Approximately 120
- Total Fat: 0g
- Cholesterol: 0mg
- Sodium: 0mg
- Total Carbohydrates: 30g
- Sugars: 30g
- Protein: 0g

Enjoy your Rockslide Rock Candy and let the flavors transport you into the heart of Jumanji's excitement!

55. Vineyard Viper Veggies

Embark on a culinary adventure inspired by the mystical world of Jumanji with our "Vineyard Viper Veggies" recipe. Just like the unpredictable twists and turns of the game itself, these delectable veggies are a wild mix of flavors and textures that will transport your taste buds to a vibrant and exotic realm. Packed with the essence of the jungle, this dish is a tribute to the magical wonders that unfold in the heart of Jumanji.

Serving: 4 servings
Preparation Time: 15 minutes
Ready Time: 30 minutes

Ingredients:
- 1 large eggplant, diced
- 1 zucchini, sliced
- 1 yellow bell pepper, sliced
- 1 red onion, thinly sliced
- 1 cup cherry tomatoes
- 1/4 cup olive oil
- 2 cloves garlic, minced
- 1 teaspoon dried oregano
- 1 teaspoon smoked paprika
- Salt and pepper to taste
- 1 tablespoon balsamic vinegar
- 2 tablespoons fresh parsley, chopped

Instructions:
1. Preheat your oven to 400°F (200°C).
2. In a large mixing bowl, combine the diced eggplant, sliced zucchini, yellow bell pepper, red onion, and cherry tomatoes.
3. In a small bowl, whisk together the olive oil, minced garlic, dried oregano, smoked paprika, salt, and pepper.
4. Pour the olive oil mixture over the vegetables and toss until evenly coated.
5. Spread the vegetables in a single layer on a baking sheet.
6. Roast in the preheated oven for 25-30 minutes or until the veggies are tender and slightly caramelized, stirring once halfway through.
7. Remove from the oven and drizzle balsamic vinegar over the roasted veggies. Toss gently to combine.
8. Sprinkle fresh parsley on top for a burst of freshness.
9. Serve the Vineyard Viper Veggies as a side dish or over couscous for a hearty main course.

Nutrition Information:
(Per Serving)
- Calories: 180
- Total Fat: 12g
- Saturated Fat: 2g
- Trans Fat: 0g
- Cholesterol: 0mg
- Sodium: 50mg
- Total Carbohydrates: 18g
- Dietary Fiber: 6g
- Sugars: 8g
- Protein: 3g

Transport yourself to the heart of Jumanji with this tantalizing dish that captures the spirit of adventure in every bite. Enjoy the Vineyard Viper Veggies with friends and family, and let the magic of Jumanji infuse your dining experience!

56. Lion's Mane Lemonade

Step into the fantastical world of Jumanji with a refreshing twist – the Lion's Mane Lemonade. Inspired by the lush and vibrant jungles of Jumanji, this unique beverage combines the earthy goodness of Lion's Mane mushrooms with the zesty kick of fresh lemons. Sip on the magic of the jungle while enjoying this enchanting concoction that brings the film to life in every sip.

Serving: Makes 4 servings
Preparation Time: 15 minutes
Ready Time: 2 hours (includes chilling time)

Ingredients:
- 1 cup Lion's Mane mushroom slices
- 4 cups water
- 1 cup fresh lemon juice
- 1/2 cup honey or maple syrup (adjust to taste)
- Ice cubes
- Lemon slices and mint leaves for garnish

Instructions:
1. In a saucepan, combine Lion's Mane mushroom slices and water. Bring to a gentle boil, then reduce heat and simmer for 10 minutes. This extracts the earthy flavors of the mushroom.
2. Remove the mushroom slices using a strainer and let the mushroom-infused water cool to room temperature.
3. In a pitcher, combine the mushroom-infused water, fresh lemon juice, and honey or maple syrup. Stir well to ensure the sweetener is fully dissolved.
4. Refrigerate the mixture for at least 2 hours to allow the flavors to meld and the lemonade to chill thoroughly.
5. Once chilled, serve the Lion's Mane Lemonade over ice cubes in glasses.
6. Garnish each glass with a slice of lemon and a sprig of mint for a touch of freshness.

Nutrition Information (per serving):
- Calories: 80
- Total Fat: 0g
- Saturated Fat: 0g
- Cholesterol: 0mg

- Sodium: 5mg
- Total Carbohydrates: 21g
- Dietary Fiber: 0.5g
- Sugars: 18g
- Protein: 0.5g

Immerse yourself in the Jumanji experience with this unique Lion's Mane Lemonade – a beverage that captures the essence of the jungle in a delightful, refreshing drink.

57. Tarzan Tart

Embark on a culinary adventure inspired by the fantastical world of Jumanji with the "Tarzan Tart." This delightful treat pays homage to the wild and untamed spirit of the jungle, capturing the essence of Tarzan's jungle abode. Packed with exotic flavors and textures, this tart is sure to transport your taste buds to the heart of the mysterious and thrilling Jumanji universe.

Serving: Makes 8 servings
Preparation Time: 20 minutes
Ready Time: 2 hours (including chilling time)

Ingredients:
For the Tart Crust:
- 1 1/2 cups graham cracker crumbs
- 1/3 cup melted butter
- 1/4 cup sugar
- A pinch of salt

For the Tarzan Tart Filling:
- 1 cup cream cheese, softened
- 1/2 cup powdered sugar
- 1 teaspoon vanilla extract
- 1 cup heavy cream, whipped
- 1 cup fresh tropical fruits (mango, pineapple, kiwi), diced

For the Jungle Drizzle:
- 1/4 cup chocolate chips
- 2 tablespoons coconut oil

Instructions:
For the Tart Crust:
1. In a bowl, combine graham cracker crumbs, melted butter, sugar, and a pinch of salt.
2. Press the mixture into the bottom of a tart pan to form an even crust.
3. Chill the crust in the refrigerator for at least 30 minutes.

For the Tarzan Tart Filling:
1. In a large bowl, beat together the cream cheese, powdered sugar, and vanilla extract until smooth and creamy.
2. Gently fold in the whipped cream until well combined.
3. Pour the filling into the chilled tart crust, spreading it evenly.
4. Top the tart with diced tropical fruits, arranging them in a visually appealing manner.

For the Jungle Drizzle:
1. In a microwave-safe bowl, melt chocolate chips and coconut oil together in 20-second intervals, stirring until smooth.
2. Drizzle the chocolate mixture over the tart, creating a wild and artistic pattern.

Chilling and Serving:
1. Place the Tarzan Tart in the refrigerator for at least 1-2 hours to set.
2. Once set, slice and serve this jungle-inspired delight to your fellow adventurers.

Nutrition Information:
(Per serving)
- Calories: 350
- Total Fat: 25g
- Saturated Fat: 15g
- Cholesterol: 60mg
- Sodium: 180mg
- Total Carbohydrates: 30g
- Dietary Fiber: 2g
- Sugars: 18g
- Protein: 4g

Immerse yourself in the Jumanji experience with every bite of this Tarzan Tart, a perfect fusion of cinematic inspiration and delectable indulgence!

58. Zebra Ziti

Embark on a culinary adventure inspired by the wild and whimsical world of Jumanji with our "Zebra Ziti" recipe. This dish pays homage to the enchanting landscapes and mysterious creatures encountered in the iconic film series. Just like the game itself, this Zebra Ziti is a blend of unexpected flavors and textures that will transport your taste buds to a world of culinary excitement.

Serving: 4-6 servings
Preparation Time: 15 minutes
Ready Time: 45 minutes

Ingredients:
- 1 pound ziti pasta
- 1 tablespoon olive oil
- 1 onion, finely chopped
- 2 cloves garlic, minced
- 1 pound ground beef or plant-based alternative
- 1 can (28 ounces) crushed tomatoes
- 1 teaspoon dried oregano
- 1 teaspoon dried basil
- 1/2 teaspoon salt
- 1/4 teaspoon black pepper
- 1 cup ricotta cheese
- 1 cup grated Parmesan cheese
- 1 1/2 cups shredded mozzarella cheese
- Fresh basil leaves for garnish (optional)

Instructions:
1. Prepare the Ziti:
- Cook the ziti pasta according to the package instructions. Drain and set aside.
2. Create the Sauce:
- In a large skillet, heat olive oil over medium heat. Add chopped onions and garlic, sautéing until softened.
- Add ground beef (or plant-based alternative) to the skillet, breaking it apart with a spatula and cooking until browned.
- Pour in the crushed tomatoes and season with oregano, basil, salt, and black pepper. Simmer for 10-15 minutes, allowing the flavors to meld.

3. Assemble the Zebra Ziti:
- Preheat the oven to 375°F (190°C).
- In a large mixing bowl, combine the cooked ziti with the meat sauce. Mix well.
- In a baking dish, layer half of the ziti mixture. Dot the surface with spoonfuls of ricotta cheese and sprinkle Parmesan and mozzarella over the layer.
- Repeat the layering process, finishing with a generous layer of mozzarella on top.
4. Bake to Perfection:
- Place the baking dish in the preheated oven and bake for 25-30 minutes or until the cheese is melted and bubbly, with a golden brown crust.
5. Garnish and Serve:
- Remove the Zebra Ziti from the oven and let it cool for a few minutes. Garnish with fresh basil leaves if desired.
- Serve hot, and let the magical flavors of the Jumanji-inspired Zebra Ziti transport you to a culinary adventure!

Nutrition Information:
(Per Serving - based on 6 servings)
- Calories: 550
- Protein: 30g
- Fat: 22g
- Carbohydrates: 55g
- Fiber: 5g
- Sugar: 8g
- Sodium: 800mg

Enjoy your journey into the heart of Jumanji with this delightful Zebra Ziti!

59. Quicksand Quinoa Salad

Step into the wild world of Jumanji with this Quicksand Quinoa Salad, inspired by the thrilling adventures and unexpected twists of the classic film. Packed with vibrant flavors and wholesome ingredients, this salad is a delicious tribute to the unpredictable journey that the characters face in the game. Get ready to embark on a culinary adventure with this quick and easy-to-make dish that will transport you to the heart of the jungle!

Serving: 4 servings
Preparation Time: 15 minutes
Ready Time: 30 minutes

Ingredients:
- 1 cup quinoa, rinsed and drained
- 2 cups water
- 1 cup cherry tomatoes, halved
- 1 cucumber, diced
- 1 red bell pepper, diced
- 1/2 red onion, finely chopped
- 1/4 cup fresh cilantro, chopped
- 1/4 cup feta cheese, crumbled
- 1/3 cup black olives, sliced
- 2 tablespoons extra-virgin olive oil
- 1 tablespoon balsamic vinegar
- 1 teaspoon Dijon mustard
- Salt and pepper to taste

Instructions:
1. Cook Quinoa:
- In a medium saucepan, combine quinoa and water. Bring to a boil, then reduce heat to low, cover, and simmer for 15 minutes, or until quinoa is cooked and water is absorbed. Fluff quinoa with a fork and let it cool to room temperature.
2. Prepare Vegetables:
- In a large bowl, combine the cooked quinoa, cherry tomatoes, cucumber, red bell pepper, red onion, cilantro, feta cheese, and black olives.
3. Make Dressing:
- In a small bowl, whisk together olive oil, balsamic vinegar, Dijon mustard, salt, and pepper.
4. Combine and Toss:
- Pour the dressing over the quinoa and vegetable mixture. Gently toss everything together until well combined.
5. Chill and Serve:
- Refrigerate the salad for at least 15 minutes to allow the flavors to meld. Serve chilled, and enjoy the delightful combination of textures and tastes.

Nutrition Information:
Per serving:
- Calories: 280
- Total Fat: 12g
- Saturated Fat: 3g
- Trans Fat: 0g
- Cholesterol: 8mg
- Sodium: 240mg
- Total Carbohydrates: 34g
- Dietary Fiber: 5g
- Sugars: 3g
- Protein: 9g

Immerse yourself in the flavors of Jumanji with this Quicksand Quinoa Salad, a dish that captures the essence of adventure in every bite. Perfect for a quick and healthy meal, it's a delightful addition to your repertoire of recipes inspired by the magic of the big screen.

60. Water Buffalo Biscuits

Embark on a culinary adventure inspired by the wild and whimsical world of Jumanji with our Water Buffalo Biscuits. These savory delights pay homage to the untamed spirit of the game, blending bold flavors and rustic charm. Get ready to roll the dice in your kitchen and create a dish that transports you straight into the heart of the jungle.

Serving: Makes approximately 12 biscuits.
Preparation Time: 15 minutes
Ready Time: 30 minutes

Ingredients:
- 2 cups all-purpose flour
- 1 tablespoon baking powder
- 1/2 teaspoon baking soda
- 1/2 teaspoon salt
- 1/2 cup unsalted butter, cold and cubed
- 1 cup buttermilk
- 1/2 cup shredded water buffalo cheese
- 1/4 cup fresh chives, finely chopped

- 1/4 cup crispy bacon, crumbled (optional, for an extra adventurous twist)

Instructions:
1. Preheat your oven to 450°F (230°C). Line a baking sheet with parchment paper.
2. In a large mixing bowl, whisk together the flour, baking powder, baking soda, and salt.
3. Add the cold, cubed butter to the dry ingredients. Using a pastry cutter or your fingertips, incorporate the butter until the mixture resembles coarse crumbs.
4. Make a well in the center of the mixture and pour in the buttermilk. Stir gently until just combined.
5. Fold in the shredded water buffalo cheese, chopped chives, and crumbled bacon (if using).
6. Turn the dough out onto a floured surface and knead it lightly, just until it comes together. Pat the dough to a 1-inch thickness.
7. Using a round biscuit cutter, cut out biscuits and place them on the prepared baking sheet.
8. Bake in the preheated oven for 12-15 minutes or until the biscuits are golden brown on top.
9. Allow the biscuits to cool for a few minutes before serving.

Nutrition Information:
(Per serving, based on 1 biscuit)
- Calories: 180
- Total Fat: 9g
- Saturated Fat: 6g
- Trans Fat: 0g
- Cholesterol: 25mg
- Sodium: 380mg
- Total Carbohydrates: 20g
- Dietary Fiber: 1g
- Sugars: 1g
- Protein: 5g

Indulge in these Water Buffalo Biscuits as you channel your inner explorer, and let the flavors transport you into the fantastical world of Jumanji. Enjoy the journey!

61. Mangrove Margarita

Embark on a culinary adventure inspired by the mystical world of Jumanji with the Mangrove Margarita. Transport yourself to the heart of the jungle with this exotic concoction that perfectly captures the spirit of the wild. This vibrant drink pays homage to the lush mangroves and untamed landscapes depicted in the film, promising a taste of the unexpected with every sip.

Serving: This recipe yields 2 servings.
Preparation Time: 15 minutes
Ready Time: 5 minutes

Ingredients:
- 2 oz silver tequila
- 1 oz triple sec
- 1 oz fresh lime juice
- 1 oz mango puree
- 1/2 oz agave syrup
- Ice cubes
- Salt (for rimming the glasses)
- Lime slices and mango wedges (for garnish)

Instructions:
1. Begin by rimming the edges of your glasses with salt. To do this, moisten the rims with a lime wedge and dip them into salt on a flat surface. Set aside.
2. In a cocktail shaker, combine the silver tequila, triple sec, fresh lime juice, mango puree, and agave syrup.
3. Add a generous amount of ice cubes to the shaker, securing the lid tightly.
4. Shake the mixture vigorously for about 10-15 seconds to ensure it's well-chilled.
5. Strain the margarita into the prepared glasses, taking care not to disturb the salted rims.
6. Garnish each glass with a slice of lime and a wedge of fresh mango for an extra tropical touch.
7. Serve immediately and enjoy the adventurous flavors of the Mangrove Margarita!

Nutrition Information (per serving):
- Calories: 210
- Total Fat: 0g
- Saturated Fat: 0g
- Cholesterol: 0mg
- Sodium: 1mg
- Total Carbohydrates: 23g
- Dietary Fiber: 1g
- Sugars: 19g
- Protein: 0g

Indulge in this tantalizing Mangrove Margarita as you journey through the pages of the Jumanji-inspired cookbook. Let the flavors transport you to the heart of the jungle, where the unexpected is always on the menu!

62. Rhino Root Beer Float

Step into the wild world of Jumanji with a tantalizing treat that captures the essence of adventure and excitement – the Rhino Root Beer Float! Inspired by the thrilling scenes of the jungle, this delightful concoction is a playful twist on the classic root beer float, combining the bold flavors of root beer with the richness of vanilla ice cream. Get ready to embark on a flavor expedition that mirrors the unpredictable twists and turns of the iconic board game. Let the Rhino Root Beer Float transport you to the heart of the Jumanji jungle, where every sip is a taste of the unexpected.

Serving: 2 servings
Preparation Time: 10 minutes
Ready Time: 10 minutes

Ingredients:
- 2 cups root beer (chilled)
- 4 scoops vanilla ice cream
- 1 tablespoon chocolate syrup
- Whipped cream (for garnish)
- Maraschino cherries (for garnish)

Instructions:
1. Chill the Glasses:
Place the glasses in the freezer for a few minutes to chill.
2. Pour Root Beer:
Divide the chilled root beer equally between the two glasses, ensuring a refreshing base for your Rhino Root Beer Float.
3. Add Ice Cream:
Carefully place two scoops of vanilla ice cream into each glass, allowing the creamy goodness to float on top of the root beer.
4. Drizzle with Chocolate Syrup:
Drizzle a tablespoon of chocolate syrup over each float, creating a decadent swirl of flavor reminiscent of the hidden treasures in the Jumanji jungle.
5. Garnish:
Top each float with a generous dollop of whipped cream and crown it with a vibrant maraschino cherry, adding a pop of color and a touch of whimsy.
6. Serve and Enjoy:
Present your Rhino Root Beer Floats with a sense of adventure. Stir with a long spoon and sip your way through the layers of root beer, velvety ice cream, and chocolatey goodness.

Nutrition Information:
Note: Nutritional values are approximate and may vary based on specific ingredients used.
- Calories: 350 per serving
- Fat: 15g
- Cholesterol: 45mg
- Sodium: 80mg
- Carbohydrates: 50g
- Sugar: 40g
- Protein: 5g

The Rhino Root Beer Float is not just a beverage; it's a cinematic experience for your taste buds. Let this sweet and fizzy creation be a highlight at your next movie night, and savor the excitement inspired by the world of Jumanji.

63. Panther Pecan Pie

Step into the wild and embark on a culinary adventure inspired by the thrilling world of Jumanji! Our "Panther Pecan Pie" pays homage to the mysterious and enchanting creatures that roam the jungle. This delectable dessert is a blend of rich flavors, capturing the essence of the untamed spirit within the Jumanji universe. Get ready to experience a taste sensation that will transport you into the heart of the jungle with every bite.

Serving: Serves 8
Preparation Time: 20 minutes
Ready Time: 1 hour and 30 minutes

Ingredients:
- 1 9-inch pie crust (store-bought or homemade)
- 1 cup pecan halves
- 1/2 cup unsalted butter, melted
- 1 cup light corn syrup
- 1 cup granulated sugar
- 3 large eggs, beaten
- 1 teaspoon vanilla extract
- 1/4 teaspoon salt
- Dark chocolate chips for garnish (optional)

Instructions:
1. Preheat your oven to 350°F (175°C).
2. In a large mixing bowl, combine the melted butter, corn syrup, sugar, beaten eggs, vanilla extract, and salt. Mix until well combined.
3. Arrange the pecan halves evenly over the bottom of the pie crust.
4. Pour the buttery filling mixture over the pecans, ensuring an even distribution.
5. If desired, sprinkle dark chocolate chips over the top for an extra indulgent touch.
6. Place the pie on a baking sheet to catch any potential spills and bake in the preheated oven for approximately 60-70 minutes, or until the center is set and a toothpick inserted comes out clean.
7. Allow the Panther Pecan Pie to cool completely on a wire rack before slicing.

8. Serve each slice with a dollop of whipped cream or a scoop of vanilla ice cream for an extra treat.

Nutrition Information:
Note: Nutrition information is per serving.
- Calories: 480
- Total Fat: 26g
- Saturated Fat: 9g
- Trans Fat: 0g
- Cholesterol: 85mg
- Sodium: 190mg
- Total Carbohydrates: 60g
- Dietary Fiber: 2g
- Sugars: 45g
- Protein: 4g

Delight your taste buds with the magic of Jumanji, and savor the wild flavors of our Panther Pecan Pie. This dessert is sure to be a showstopper at your next gathering, transporting everyone to a world of adventure and excitement.

64. Python Pumpkin Pancakes

Embark on a culinary adventure inspired by the enchanting world of Jumanji with our delightful "Python Pumpkin Pancakes." These pancakes pay homage to the film's wild and mysterious spirit, blending the warmth of pumpkin with the adventurous twist of Python spices. Get ready to savor a breakfast experience that brings the jungle to your plate!

Serving: Makes approximately 8 pancakes.
Preparation Time: 15 minutes
Ready Time: 30 minutes

Ingredients:
- 1 cup all-purpose flour
- 1/4 cup python spice blend (cinnamon, nutmeg, and ginger)
- 1 teaspoon baking powder
- 1/2 teaspoon baking soda
- 1/4 teaspoon salt

- 1 cup pumpkin puree
- 1 cup buttermilk
- 2 large eggs
- 2 tablespoons melted butter
- 2 tablespoons maple syrup
- 1 teaspoon vanilla extract
- Butter or cooking spray for the pan

Instructions:
1. In a large mixing bowl, combine the flour, python spice blend, baking powder, baking soda, and salt. Whisk together until well incorporated.
2. In another bowl, whisk together the pumpkin puree, buttermilk, eggs, melted butter, maple syrup, and vanilla extract.
3. Pour the wet ingredients into the dry ingredients and gently fold until just combined. Be careful not to overmix; a few lumps are okay.
4. Heat a skillet or griddle over medium heat and lightly grease with butter or cooking spray.
5. Pour 1/4 cup of batter onto the hot skillet for each pancake. Cook until bubbles form on the surface, then flip and cook the other side until golden brown.
6. Repeat until all the batter is used, keeping the cooked pancakes warm.
7. Serve the Python Pumpkin Pancakes with a drizzle of maple syrup and a sprinkle of extra python spice for an extra kick.

Nutrition Information:
Per serving (2 pancakes):
- Calories: 280
- Total Fat: 10g
- Saturated Fat: 5g
- Cholesterol: 90mg
- Sodium: 400mg
- Total Carbohydrates: 40g
- Dietary Fiber: 3g
- Sugars: 10g
- Protein: 7g

Indulge in the flavors of Jumanji with these Python Pumpkin Pancakes, a perfect blend of cinematic inspiration and delicious breakfast delight!

65. Baboon BBQ Ribs

Transport yourself to the heart of the Jumanji jungle with these succulent Baboon BBQ Ribs. Inspired by the wild adventures in the iconic film, these ribs promise to bring the spirit of the game to your dinner table. Marinated in a flavorful blend of spices and slow-cooked to perfection, these ribs are a true delight for the senses. Gather your fellow adventurers and get ready for a culinary journey through the untamed flavors of Jumanji.

Serving: 4-6 people
Preparation Time: 15 minutes
Ready Time: 4 hours (including marination and cooking)

Ingredients:
- 2 racks of baby back ribs
- 1 cup BBQ sauce
- 1/4 cup soy sauce
- 1/4 cup honey
- 2 tablespoons brown sugar
- 1 tablespoon Dijon mustard
- 1 tablespoon paprika
- 1 teaspoon garlic powder
- 1 teaspoon onion powder
- 1 teaspoon ground cumin
- Salt and black pepper to taste

Instructions:
1. Prep the Ribs:
- Remove the membrane from the back of the ribs for a tender texture.
- Season the ribs generously with salt and black pepper.
2. Prepare the Marinade:
- In a bowl, combine BBQ sauce, soy sauce, honey, brown sugar, Dijon mustard, paprika, garlic powder, onion powder, and ground cumin.
- Mix well until the sugar is dissolved and the ingredients are thoroughly combined.
3. Marinate the Ribs:
- Place the ribs in a large resealable plastic bag or a shallow dish.
- Pour half of the marinade over the ribs, ensuring they are well-coated.

- Seal the bag or cover the dish and refrigerate for at least 2 hours, or preferably overnight, to let the flavors meld.

4. Preheat the Grill or Oven:
- Preheat your grill or oven to medium heat (about 300°F/150°C).

5. Cook the Ribs:
- If using a grill, place the ribs on the preheated grill and cook for 2-2.5 hours, turning occasionally and basting with the remaining marinade.
- If using an oven, place the ribs on a baking sheet lined with aluminum foil and bake for 2-2.5 hours at 300°F/150°C, turning and basting halfway through.

6. Check for Doneness:
- The ribs are done when the meat is tender and easily pulls away from the bone.

7. Serve:
- Transfer the Baboon BBQ Ribs to a serving platter.
- Garnish with chopped fresh cilantro or green onions for a touch of freshness.

Nutrition Information:
Note: Nutritional values may vary depending on specific ingredients and portion sizes.
- Calories: approximately 450 per serving
- Protein: 25g
- Fat: 20g
- Carbohydrates: 40g
- Fiber: 2g

Bring the wild flavors of Jumanji to life with these Baboon BBQ Ribs, a perfect blend of sweet, savory, and smoky goodness that will leave your taste buds roaring for more.

66. Elephant Endive Wraps

Step into the wild and adventurous world of Jumanji with these Elephant Endive Wraps! Inspired by the lush and exotic setting of the film, these wraps are a flavorful journey for your taste buds. Packed with vibrant ingredients and a touch of mystery, they're the perfect addition to your culinary escapades. Get ready to embark on a taste adventure!

Serving: Makes 4 servings.
Preparation Time: 20 minutes.
Ready Time: 20 minutes.

Ingredients:
- 1 lb ground elephant yam
- 1 cup cooked quinoa
- 1 cup diced exotic fruits (mango, pineapple, kiwi)
- 1/2 cup chopped water chestnuts
- 1/4 cup chopped cilantro
- 1/4 cup chopped mint
- 1/4 cup chopped roasted peanuts
- 1/4 cup sesame oil
- 2 tablespoons soy sauce
- 1 tablespoon honey
- 1 tablespoon rice vinegar
- 1 teaspoon grated ginger
- 1 teaspoon minced garlic
- Salt and pepper to taste
- 12-16 large endive leaves, washed and separated

Instructions:
1. In a large pan, sauté the ground elephant yam over medium heat until cooked through. Set aside to cool.
2. In a large mixing bowl, combine the cooked quinoa, diced exotic fruits, water chestnuts, cilantro, mint, and roasted peanuts.
3. In a small bowl, whisk together sesame oil, soy sauce, honey, rice vinegar, grated ginger, minced garlic, salt, and pepper. Pour the dressing over the quinoa mixture and toss until well combined.
4. Add the cooked elephant yam to the bowl and mix thoroughly.
5. Spoon the mixture onto each endive leaf, creating flavorful and colorful wraps.
6. Arrange the Elephant Endive Wraps on a serving platter and garnish with additional cilantro and mint if desired.

Nutrition Information:
Note: Nutritional values are approximate and may vary based on specific ingredients used.
- Calories: 300 per serving
- Protein: 8g

- Carbohydrates: 35g
- Fat: 15g
- Fiber: 6g
- Sugar: 8g
- Sodium: 450mg

These Elephant Endive Wraps are not only a feast for the senses but also a nod to the wild, untamed spirit of Jumanji. Enjoy this exotic and flavorful dish that brings the jungle to your table!

67. Monkey Mango Salsa

Embark on a flavorful journey through the dense jungles of Jumanji with our delightful Monkey Mango Salsa. Inspired by the vibrant and unpredictable world of the film, this salsa combines the sweetness of ripe mangoes with a hint of spice to create a tantalizing taste experience. Whether you're a seasoned explorer or a casual adventurer, this Monkey Mango Salsa will transport your taste buds to the heart of the jungle.

Serving: Ideal for 4-6 servings.
Preparation Time: 15 minutes
Ready Time: 15 minutes

Ingredients:
- 2 ripe mangoes, peeled, pitted, and diced
- 1 cup diced fresh pineapple
- 1/2 cup red bell pepper, finely diced
- 1/4 cup red onion, finely chopped
- 1 jalapeño pepper, seeds removed and finely minced
- 1/4 cup fresh cilantro, chopped
- Juice of 2 limes
- Salt and pepper to taste

Instructions:
1. In a large mixing bowl, combine the diced mangoes, fresh pineapple, red bell pepper, red onion, and jalapeño pepper.
2. Gently fold in the chopped cilantro, ensuring an even distribution of flavors.

3. Squeeze the lime juice over the mixture, and toss the ingredients together until well combined.
4. Season the salsa with salt and pepper to taste, adjusting the quantities based on your preference for sweetness and spice.
5. Allow the salsa to marinate for at least 10 minutes, allowing the flavors to meld together.
6. Serve the Monkey Mango Salsa chilled with tortilla chips, as a topping for grilled chicken or fish, or as a refreshing side dish.

Nutrition Information:
(Per Serving)
- Calories: 90 kcal
- Total Fat: 0.5g
- Saturated Fat: 0g
- Cholesterol: 0mg
- Sodium: 5mg
- Total Carbohydrates: 22g
- Dietary Fiber: 3g
- Sugars: 17g
- Protein: 1g

Dive into the exotic flavors of the jungle with Monkey Mango Salsa, a delightful homage to the cinematic wonders of Jumanji. This vibrant concoction is sure to add a burst of tropical goodness to your culinary adventures.

68. Leopard Lollipop

Step into the wild world of Jumanji with the exciting and delectable "Leopard Lollipop." Inspired by the vibrant and untamed spirit of the film, this treat is not only a visual delight but also a scrumptious adventure for your taste buds. Channel your inner explorer and embark on a culinary journey with this playful and delicious recipe that brings the magic of Jumanji to your table.

Serving: Makes 12 Leopard Lollipops
Preparation Time: 20 minutes
Ready Time: 2 hours (including chilling time)

Ingredients:
- 2 cups white chocolate chips
- 1 tablespoon coconut oil
- 12 lollipop sticks
- Assorted food coloring (black, orange, and brown)
- 1/4 cup dark chocolate chips (for eyes)
- 1 tablespoon vegetable shortening

Instructions:
1. Prepare a Baking Sheet:
Line a baking sheet with parchment paper and set aside.
2. Melt White Chocolate:
In a microwave-safe bowl, melt the white chocolate chips and coconut oil in 30-second intervals, stirring after each, until smooth and fully melted.
3. Divide Chocolate:
Divide the melted white chocolate into three separate bowls.
4. Add Food Coloring:
In one bowl, add black food coloring to create the spots of the leopard. In another bowl, add orange food coloring for the base color of the leopard, and in the third bowl, add brown food coloring for additional spots.
5. Create Leopard Patterns:
Take each lollipop stick and dip it into the orange chocolate, leaving some space at the top for the ears. Place the dipped sticks onto the prepared baking sheet.
6. Add Spots:
Using a spoon or piping bag, add black and brown spots onto the orange chocolate to create the leopard pattern. Be creative with the placement of spots to mimic the wild and untamed look.
7. Create Ears:
Using the remaining orange chocolate, create small rounded shapes at the top of each lollipop to resemble leopard ears.
8. Add Eyes:
Melt the dark chocolate chips with vegetable shortening and use it to add eyes to each leopard lollipop.
9. Chill:
Place the baking sheet in the refrigerator for at least 2 hours to allow the chocolate to set.
10. Serve:

Once the chocolate is fully set, your Leopard Lollipops are ready to be enjoyed. Serve them at your Jumanji-inspired gathering and watch as they disappear into the mouths of adventurers young and old!

Nutrition Information:
(Per Serving)
- Calories: 180
- Total Fat: 12g
- Saturated Fat: 8g
- Cholesterol: 5mg
- Sodium: 20mg
- Total Carbohydrates: 18g
- Dietary Fiber: 1g
- Sugars: 15g
- Protein: 2g

Note: Nutrition information is approximate and may vary based on specific ingredients used.

69. Cobra Coconut Curry

Transport your taste buds on a wild adventure inspired by the untamed world of Jumanji with this exotic Cobra Coconut Curry. A fusion of vibrant flavors and aromatic spices, this dish captures the essence of the jungle in every bite. Get ready for a culinary journey that mirrors the excitement of the iconic film Jumanji, where danger and delight await at every turn. Embrace the thrill and savor the magic of Cobra Coconut Curry!

Serving: 4 servings
Preparation Time: 15 minutes
Ready Time: 45 minutes

Ingredients:
- 1 lb cobra meat, thinly sliced (substitute with chicken or tofu for a tamer version)
- 2 tbsp vegetable oil
- 1 large onion, finely chopped
- 3 cloves garlic, minced

- 1 tbsp ginger, grated
- 2 tbsp red curry paste
- 1 can (14 oz) coconut milk
- 1 cup bamboo shoots, sliced
- 1 cup bell peppers, thinly sliced
- 1 cup baby corn, halved
- 1 cup snap peas
- 1 tbsp fish sauce
- 1 tbsp soy sauce
- 1 tbsp brown sugar
- Fresh cilantro leaves for garnish
- Cooked jasmine rice for serving

Instructions:
1. Heat vegetable oil in a large pan over medium heat. Add chopped onions and cook until translucent.
2. Stir in minced garlic and grated ginger, sautéing until fragrant.
3. Add red curry paste to the pan, stirring well to combine with the aromatics.
4. Incorporate thinly sliced cobra meat into the mixture, cooking until browned on all sides.
5. Pour in coconut milk, stirring continuously to create a rich and creamy curry base.
6. Add bamboo shoots, bell peppers, baby corn, and snap peas to the pan. Allow the vegetables to simmer in the flavorful broth.
7. Season the curry with fish sauce, soy sauce, and brown sugar, adjusting to taste.
8. Simmer the Cobra Coconut Curry for 30-40 minutes, allowing the flavors to meld together and the sauce to thicken.
9. Serve the curry over a bed of jasmine rice, garnishing with fresh cilantro leaves.

Nutrition Information (per serving):
- Calories: 450
- Protein: 25g
- Fat: 30g
- Carbohydrates: 20g
- Fiber: 5g
- Sugar: 8g
- Sodium: 800mg

Embark on a culinary quest with this Cobra Coconut Curry, a dish that pays homage to the adventurous spirit of Jumanji. Let the flavors transport you to the heart of the jungle, where danger and delight collide in a symphony of taste.

70. Crocodile Crème Brûlée

Embark on a culinary adventure inspired by the wild and untamed world of Jumanji with our exotic twist on the classic Crème Brûlée. The Crocodile Crème Brûlée is a daring fusion of creamy indulgence and adventurous flavors, transporting you to the heart of the jungle with every decadent bite. This dessert is a nod to the unpredictable nature of Jumanji, where surprises await at every turn.

Serving: 4 servings
Preparation Time: 20 minutes
Ready Time: 4 hours (includes chilling time)

Ingredients:
- 4 crocodile egg yolks
- 1/2 cup granulated sugar
- 2 cups heavy cream
- 1 vanilla bean, split and seeds scraped
- 1/4 teaspoon salt
- 4 tablespoons brown sugar (for caramelizing)

Instructions:
1. Preheat Oven:
Preheat your oven to 325°F (163°C).
2. Prepare Crocodile Eggs:
Carefully separate the crocodile egg yolks from the whites, ensuring no traces of egg whites remain in the yolks.
3. Mix Sugar and Crocodile Yolks:
In a mixing bowl, whisk together the crocodile egg yolks and granulated sugar until the mixture becomes pale and slightly thickened.
4. Heat Cream and Vanilla:

In a saucepan over medium heat, combine the heavy cream, vanilla bean seeds, and salt. Heat until it just begins to simmer. Remove from heat and let it sit for a few minutes to infuse the vanilla flavor.

5. Temper the Eggs:

Slowly pour the warm cream mixture into the crocodile egg mixture, whisking constantly to temper the eggs. This prevents the eggs from scrambling.

6. Strain the Mixture:

Strain the custard mixture through a fine-mesh sieve into a bowl to remove any lumps or solid bits.

7. Prepare Ramekins:

Place four ramekins in a baking dish. Pour the custard mixture evenly into the ramekins.

8. Bake in Water Bath:

Pour hot water into the baking dish to create a water bath around the ramekins. Bake in the preheated oven for about 30-35 minutes or until the edges are set, but the center is slightly jiggly.

9. Chill:

Remove the ramekins from the water bath and let them cool. Refrigerate for at least 3 hours or overnight until fully chilled.

10. Caramelize the Top:

Just before serving, sprinkle a thin, even layer of brown sugar on top of each custard. Use a kitchen torch to caramelize the sugar until golden and crispy.

11. Serve:

Allow the caramel to harden for a minute, then serve your Crocodile Crème Brûlée immediately, capturing the essence of Jumanji in each delightful spoonful.

Nutrition Information:
(Per serving)
- Calories: 420
- Fat: 35g
- Saturated Fat: 21g
- Cholesterol: 340mg
- Sodium: 150mg
- Carbohydrates: 23g
- Sugar: 21g
- Protein: 5g

Dare to venture into the unknown with this daring dessert inspired by the mysteries of Jumanji. The Crocodile Crème Brûlée promises a taste journey like no other, blending the richness of traditional custard with the thrill of the unexpected.

71. Tiger Tail Tarts

Embark on a culinary adventure inspired by the wild and whimsical world of Jumanji with our Tiger Tail Tarts. These delightful treats pay homage to the exotic and untamed spirit of the jungle, bringing a touch of magic to your table. Get ready to indulge in a sweet escape that captures the essence of this beloved film. Brace yourself for a taste journey as thrilling as the game itself!

Serving: Makes 12 Tiger Tail Tarts
Preparation Time: 20 minutes
Ready Time: 45 minutes

Ingredients:
- 1 package of pre-made puff pastry sheets
- 1/2 cup tiger nut butter
- 1/4 cup honey
- 1/4 cup shredded coconut
- 1/4 cup crushed pineapple, drained
- 1/4 cup chopped macadamia nuts
- 1 teaspoon vanilla extract
- Pinch of salt
- 1 egg (for egg wash)

Instructions:
1. Preheat the Oven:
Preheat your oven to 375°F (190°C). Line a baking sheet with parchment paper.
2. Prepare the Pastry:
Roll out the puff pastry sheets on a floured surface. Using a round cutter, cut out 12 circles and place them on the prepared baking sheet.
3. Create the Filling:

In a bowl, mix tiger nut butter, honey, shredded coconut, crushed pineapple, chopped macadamia nuts, vanilla extract, and a pinch of salt. Ensure all ingredients are well combined.

4. Fill the Pastry:

Spoon a generous dollop of the filling onto the center of each pastry circle. Leave a small border around the edges.

5. Form the Tarts:

Fold the pastry over the filling, creating a half-moon shape. Press the edges with a fork to seal the tarts.

6. Egg Wash:

Beat the egg and brush it over the tops of the tarts for a golden finish.

7. Bake:

Bake in the preheated oven for 20-25 minutes or until the tarts are golden brown and puffed up.

8. Cool:

Allow the Tiger Tail Tarts to cool on the baking sheet for 10 minutes before transferring them to a wire rack to cool completely.

9. Serve and Enjoy:

Serve these Jumanji-inspired Tiger Tail Tarts at room temperature and immerse yourself in the magical flavors of the jungle.

Nutrition Information:

Note: Nutritional values are approximate and may vary based on specific ingredients used.

- Calories per serving: 220
- Total Fat: 15g
- Saturated Fat: 5g
- Trans Fat: 0g
- Cholesterol: 15mg
- Sodium: 120mg
- Total Carbohydrates: 18g
- Dietary Fiber: 2g
- Sugars: 6g
- Protein: 4g

Dive into these Tiger Tail Tarts and let the taste of Jumanji transport you to a world of flavor and fun!

72. Jungle Jam

Step into the enchanting world of Jumanji with this delightful and exotic Jungle Jam! Inspired by the wild and unpredictable nature of the film, this unique recipe combines vibrant tropical flavors to transport your taste buds on a thrilling adventure. Whether you're a fan of the classic Jumanji or the modern adaptations, this Jungle Jam is sure to be a hit at your next gathering.

Serving: 8 servings
Preparation Time: 15 minutes
Ready Time: 2 hours (including chilling time)

Ingredients:
- 3 cups mixed tropical fruits (such as pineapple, mango, kiwi, and passion fruit), diced
- 1 cup berries (strawberries, blueberries, or raspberries)
- 1 banana, sliced
- 1/4 cup fresh mint leaves, chopped
- 1/4 cup shredded coconut
- 1/2 cup pineapple juice
- 2 tablespoons honey
- 1 tablespoon lime juice
- 1 teaspoon grated ginger
- 1/2 teaspoon vanilla extract

Instructions:
1. In a large mixing bowl, combine the diced tropical fruits, berries, sliced banana, chopped mint leaves, and shredded coconut.
2. In a separate bowl, whisk together the pineapple juice, honey, lime juice, grated ginger, and vanilla extract to create the flavorful dressing.
3. Pour the dressing over the fruit mixture and gently toss until all the fruits are evenly coated.
4. Cover the bowl with plastic wrap and refrigerate for at least 2 hours to allow the flavors to meld and intensify.
5. Before serving, give the Jungle Jam a final toss and adjust the sweetness or acidity to your liking.
6. Spoon the Jungle Jam into individual serving bowls or glasses, garnish with additional mint leaves and shredded coconut if desired.
7. Serve chilled and enjoy the explosion of tropical flavors in every bite!

Nutrition Information (per serving):
- Calories: 120
- Total Fat: 2g
- Saturated Fat: 1.5g
- Cholesterol: 0mg
- Sodium: 5mg
- Total Carbohydrates: 28g
- Dietary Fiber: 4g
- Sugars: 20g
- Protein: 1g

Note: Nutrition information is approximate and may vary based on specific ingredients used. Adjustments can be made based on dietary preferences or restrictions.

73. Quicksand Quail Eggs

Embark on a culinary adventure inspired by the mystical world of Jumanji with these Quicksand Quail Eggs. Transport yourself to the heart of the jungle with this exotic dish that captures the essence of the film's thrilling landscapes and magical encounters. The combination of delicate quail eggs and a unique quicksand-inspired presentation will make this dish a showstopper at your table, bringing the spirit of Jumanji to life.

Serving: Ideal for a whimsical dinner party or as a captivating appetizer, this recipe serves 4.
Preparation Time: 20 minutes
Ready Time: 30 minutes

Ingredients:
- 20 quail eggs
- 1 cup breadcrumbs
- 1/2 cup all-purpose flour
- 2 large eggs, beaten
- Salt and pepper to taste
- Vegetable oil for frying
- 1 cup black sesame seeds (for the "quicksand" coating)

Instructions:
1. Prepare the Quail Eggs:
Gently place the quail eggs in a saucepan and cover them with water. Bring the water to a boil and let the eggs cook for 3-4 minutes. Once done, transfer the eggs to an ice bath to cool. Peel the quail eggs carefully and set them aside.
2. Coat the Eggs:
In three separate bowls, place the flour, beaten eggs, and breadcrumbs. Roll each quail egg in the flour, then dip it in the beaten eggs, and finally coat it with breadcrumbs.
3. Create the Quicksand Coating:
In a separate bowl, mix the black sesame seeds. Roll each breadcrumb-coated quail egg in the sesame seed mixture until fully covered, resembling the appearance of quicksand.
4. Fry the Quail Eggs:
Heat vegetable oil in a deep pan to 350°F (175°C). Carefully fry the quail eggs in batches until they turn golden brown, ensuring an even coating. Remove and drain on paper towels.
5. Serve:
Arrange the Quicksand Quail Eggs on a serving platter, creating a visually stunning display. Pair them with a dipping sauce of your choice or enjoy them on their own.

Nutrition Information:
(Per serving)
- Calories: 220
- Fat: 12g
- Saturated Fat: 2g
- Cholesterol: 380mg
- Sodium: 120mg
- Carbohydrates: 20g
- Fiber: 2g
- Protein: 8g

Transport your taste buds to the magical world of Jumanji with this unique and delicious Quicksand Quail Eggs recipe. A perfect blend of flavors and textures, this dish is sure to be a hit with both adventurous eaters and fans of the film alike.

74. Vulture Vegetable Stir-fry

Step into the wild world of Jumanji with this exotic and adventurous Vulture Vegetable Stir-fry. Inspired by the lush and untamed landscapes of the film, this dish combines a variety of vibrant vegetables to create a flavorful and visually stunning experience. Embrace the spirit of the jungle as you prepare and enjoy this unique stir-fry that captures the essence of Jumanji.

Serving: 4 servings
Preparation Time: 15 minutes
Ready Time: 25 minutes

Ingredients:
- 1 lb (450g) boneless, skinless chicken breasts, thinly sliced
- 2 tablespoons vegetable oil
- 1 red bell pepper, thinly sliced
- 1 yellow bell pepper, thinly sliced
- 1 cup (150g) snap peas, ends trimmed
- 1 cup (150g) baby corn, halved
- 1 cup (150g) water chestnuts, sliced
- 3 green onions, sliced
- 3 cloves garlic, minced
- 1 tablespoon ginger, grated
- 1/4 cup (60ml) soy sauce
- 2 tablespoons oyster sauce
- 1 tablespoon hoisin sauce
- 1 teaspoon sesame oil
- 1 teaspoon cornstarch
- 1/2 teaspoon red pepper flakes (optional)
- Cooked white rice for serving

Instructions:
1. In a small bowl, whisk together the soy sauce, oyster sauce, hoisin sauce, sesame oil, cornstarch, and red pepper flakes. Set aside.
2. Heat 1 tablespoon of vegetable oil in a wok or large skillet over medium-high heat. Add the sliced chicken and cook until browned and cooked through. Remove the chicken from the wok and set aside.

3. In the same wok, add another tablespoon of vegetable oil. Add the minced garlic and grated ginger, sautéing for about 30 seconds until fragrant.
4. Add the sliced bell peppers, snap peas, baby corn, and water chestnuts to the wok. Stir-fry for 3-4 minutes until the vegetables are crisp-tender.
5. Return the cooked chicken to the wok, along with the sliced green onions. Pour the prepared sauce over the ingredients and toss everything together until well-coated and heated through.
6. Serve the Vulture Vegetable Stir-fry over cooked white rice.

Nutrition Information:
(Per serving)
- Calories: 350
- Protein: 25g
- Fat: 12g
- Carbohydrates: 30g
- Fiber: 5g
- Sugar: 8g
- Sodium: 900mg

Immerse yourself in the flavors of Jumanji with this Vulture Vegetable Stir-fry that brings the jungle to your dinner table. Enjoy the adventure!

75. Python Pita Pockets

Embark on a culinary adventure inspired by the wild and enchanting world of Jumanji with our "Python Pita Pockets" recipe. These delightful pockets pay homage to the jungle's mysterious inhabitants and are sure to transport your taste buds on a thrilling journey.

Serving: 4 servings
Preparation Time: 15 minutes
Ready Time: 25 minutes

Ingredients:
- 1 lb python meat, diced (substitute with chicken or turkey if python is unavailable)
- 4 whole wheat pita bread pockets
- 1 cup Greek yogurt

- 1 cucumber, finely diced
- 1 tomato, diced
- 1/2 red onion, thinly sliced
- 2 cloves garlic, minced
- 1 teaspoon ground cumin
- 1 teaspoon smoked paprika
- 1/2 teaspoon coriander powder
- Salt and pepper to taste
- Fresh cilantro, chopped (for garnish)
- Olive oil for cooking

Instructions:
1. Prepare the Python (or substitute meat):
- In a skillet, heat olive oil over medium heat.
- Add diced python meat (or chicken/turkey) and cook until browned and cooked through.
- Season with salt, pepper, ground cumin, smoked paprika, and coriander powder.
- Once cooked, set aside.
2. Prepare the Pockets:
- Gently warm the whole wheat pita bread in a dry skillet or microwave for about 30 seconds to make them pliable.
- Carefully open each pita pocket, creating a small pocket for the filling.
3. Assemble the Filling:
- In a bowl, mix Greek yogurt, minced garlic, diced cucumber, diced tomato, and thinly sliced red onion.
- Add the cooked python meat (or substitute) to the mixture and stir until well combined.
4. Fill the Pockets:
- Spoon the filling mixture into each pita pocket, ensuring an even distribution of meat and vegetables.
5. Garnish and Serve:
- Garnish with fresh chopped cilantro.
- Serve the Python Pita Pockets warm and enjoy the taste of adventure!

Nutrition Information:
(Per Serving)
- Calories: 350
- Protein: 25g
- Carbohydrates: 30g

- Fat: 15g
- Fiber: 5g
- Sugar: 6g
- Sodium: 500mg

Embark on this culinary journey inspired by Jumanji, and let the flavors of Python Pita Pockets transport you to the heart of the jungle!

76. Hyena Honey Glazed Ham

Embark on a culinary adventure inspired by the fantastical world of Jumanji with our Hyena Honey Glazed Ham. This savory-sweet dish captures the essence of the wild and mysterious, bringing the flavors of the jungle straight to your table. The perfect blend of honey and spices creates a glaze that will transport your taste buds to the heart of the game. Get ready to experience a taste sensation that echoes the excitement and unpredictability of Jumanji!

Serving: Serves 8-10
Preparation Time: 15 minutes
Ready Time: 2 hours 30 minutes

Ingredients:
- 1 spiral-cut ham (approximately 8-10 pounds)
- 1 cup honey
- 1/2 cup Dijon mustard
- 1/4 cup soy sauce
- 1/4 cup orange juice
- 2 cloves garlic, minced
- 1 teaspoon ground ginger
- 1/2 teaspoon black pepper
- 1/4 teaspoon cayenne pepper (adjust to taste)
- Fresh thyme sprigs for garnish (optional)

Instructions:
1. Preheat the Oven:
Preheat your oven to 325°F (163°C).
2. Prepare the Glaze:

In a small saucepan, combine honey, Dijon mustard, soy sauce, orange juice, minced garlic, ground ginger, black pepper, and cayenne pepper. Stir well and bring to a simmer over medium heat. Allow the glaze to simmer for 5-7 minutes, stirring occasionally, until it thickens slightly.

3. Score the Ham:

Place the spiral-cut ham in a roasting pan. Score the ham by making diagonal cuts about 1 inch apart across the entire surface.

4. Glaze the Ham:

Brush the ham with the prepared glaze, making sure to get the glaze in between the slices. Reserve some glaze for basting during cooking.

5. Bake:

Cover the ham with foil and bake in the preheated oven for 1 hour. Every 30 minutes, baste the ham with the reserved glaze.

6. Final Glazing:

After 1 hour, remove the foil and brush the ham with the remaining glaze. Continue baking uncovered for an additional 30-45 minutes or until the ham is golden brown and caramelized.

7. Rest and Garnish:

Remove the ham from the oven and let it rest for 15 minutes before slicing. Optionally, garnish with fresh thyme sprigs for a touch of herbal fragrance.

8. Serve:

Slice the Hyena Honey Glazed Ham and serve it warm. Enjoy the rich, sweet, and savory flavors inspired by the magical world of Jumanji!

Nutrition Information:

(Per Serving - assuming 8 servings)

- Calories: 650
- Protein: 42g
- Total Fat: 30g
- Saturated Fat: 10g
- Cholesterol: 120mg
- Carbohydrates: 50g
- Fiber: 1g
- Sugars: 45g
- Sodium: 1800mg

Note: Nutrition information may vary based on the specific ingredients and brands used.

77. Water Buffalo Blueberry Muffins

Embark on a culinary adventure inspired by the wild and magical world of Jumanji with these Water Buffalo Blueberry Muffins. Just like the unpredictable twists and turns in the game, these muffins offer a delightful surprise with the addition of water buffalo milk. Combined with the burst of flavor from fresh blueberries, these muffins are a unique treat that captures the essence of Jumanji in every bite.

Serving: Makes 12 muffins
Preparation Time: 15 minutes
Ready Time: 35 minutes

Ingredients:
- 1 1/2 cups all-purpose flour
- 1/2 cup whole wheat flour
- 1 cup sugar
- 1 teaspoon baking powder
- 1/2 teaspoon baking soda
- 1/2 teaspoon salt
- 1/2 cup unsalted butter, melted
- 1 cup water buffalo milk
- 1 large egg
- 1 teaspoon vanilla extract
- 1 1/2 cups fresh blueberries

Instructions:
1. Preheat the oven to 375°F (190°C). Line a muffin tin with paper liners or grease each cup.
2. In a large bowl, whisk together the all-purpose flour, whole wheat flour, sugar, baking powder, baking soda, and salt.
3. In a separate bowl, combine the melted butter, water buffalo milk, egg, and vanilla extract. Mix well.
4. Pour the wet ingredients into the dry ingredients and stir until just combined. Be careful not to overmix; a few lumps are okay.
5. Gently fold in the fresh blueberries, ensuring even distribution throughout the batter.
6. Spoon the batter into the prepared muffin cups, filling each about two-thirds full.

7. Bake for 18-20 minutes or until a toothpick inserted into the center comes out clean.
8. Allow the muffins to cool in the tin for 5 minutes before transferring them to a wire rack to cool completely.

Nutrition Information:
Per Serving (1 muffin):
- Calories: 220
- Total Fat: 9g
- Saturated Fat: 5g
- Trans Fat: 0g
- Cholesterol: 35mg
- Sodium: 200mg
- Total Carbohydrates: 32g
- Dietary Fiber: 2g
- Sugars: 18g
- Protein: 3g

Delve into the fantastical flavors of Jumanji with these Water Buffalo Blueberry Muffins – a culinary ode to the unpredictable journey of the game. These muffins are sure to transport you to a world of delicious excitement!

78. Rhino Raspberry Ripple Ice Cream

Embark on a wild culinary adventure inspired by the fantastical world of Jumanji with our Rhino Raspberry Ripple Ice Cream. This delectable treat pays homage to the thrilling and unpredictable nature of the jungle, featuring the bold flavors of ripe raspberries swirled into a rich and creamy base. Whether you're a seasoned explorer or a culinary enthusiast, this dessert is sure to transport your taste buds to the heart of the Jumanji jungle.

Serving: 4 servings
Preparation Time: 15 minutes
Ready Time: 6 hours (including freezing time)

Ingredients:
- 2 cups fresh raspberries

- 1/2 cup sugar
- 1 tablespoon lemon juice
- 2 cups heavy cream
- 1 cup whole milk
- 3/4 cup granulated sugar
- 1 teaspoon vanilla extract

Instructions:
1. Prepare the Raspberry Ripple:
- In a saucepan, combine fresh raspberries, sugar, and lemon juice.
- Cook over medium heat, stirring occasionally, until the raspberries break down and the mixture thickens (about 8-10 minutes).
- Remove from heat and strain the mixture through a fine-mesh sieve to remove seeds. Allow the raspberry sauce to cool.
2. Make the Ice Cream Base:
- In a mixing bowl, whisk together heavy cream, whole milk, granulated sugar, and vanilla extract until the sugar is dissolved.
3. Combine and Chill:
- Gently fold the raspberry sauce into the ice cream base, creating a ripple effect.
- Cover the bowl and refrigerate the mixture for at least 4 hours or overnight to allow the flavors to meld.
4. Churn the Ice Cream:
- Transfer the chilled mixture to an ice cream maker and churn according to the manufacturer's instructions until it reaches a soft-serve consistency.
5. Create the Ripple Effect:
- Spoon the partially churned ice cream into a lidded container, alternating with drizzles of the remaining raspberry sauce.
- Use a knife to swirl the raspberry sauce through the ice cream, creating a ripple effect.
6. Freeze:
- Place the container in the freezer and allow the ice cream to firm up for at least 4 hours or until it reaches your desired consistency.
7. Serve:
- Scoop the Rhino Raspberry Ripple Ice Cream into bowls or cones, and indulge in a taste of Jumanji-inspired sweetness.

Nutrition Information:
(Per serving)

- Calories: 350
- Fat: 25g
- Saturated Fat: 15g
- Cholesterol: 80mg
- Sodium: 45mg
- Carbohydrates: 30g
- Fiber: 4g
- Sugars: 25g
- Protein: 3g

Now, sit back, relax, and enjoy the magic of Jumanji with each delightful spoonful of this Rhino Raspberry Ripple Ice Cream!

79. Leopard Lime Lollipops

Embark on a culinary adventure inspired by the fantastical world of Jumanji with these delightful Leopard Lime Lollipops. Just like the unpredictable twists and turns of the game, these lollipops bring a burst of vibrant flavors to your taste buds. The combination of zesty lime and playful leopard spots will transport you to the heart of the jungle, making every bite an exciting experience.

Serving: Makes approximately 12 lollipops
Preparation Time: 20 minutes
Ready Time: 2 hours (including chilling time)

Ingredients:
- 2 cups granulated sugar
- 2/3 cup water
- 1/2 cup corn syrup
- 1 teaspoon lime zest
- 1/4 cup fresh lime juice
- 1/4 teaspoon green food coloring
- Leopard Print Decorations:
- 1/4 cup dark chocolate chips, melted
- 1/4 cup white chocolate chips, melted

Instructions:
1. Prepare the Lollipop Mixture:

- In a medium saucepan, combine sugar, water, and corn syrup. Stir over medium heat until the sugar dissolves.
- Bring the mixture to a boil, then reduce the heat to medium-low and insert a candy thermometer.
- Cook the syrup without stirring until it reaches 300°F (hard crack stage).
- Remove from heat and let it cool for a few moments.

2. Add Lime Flavor:
- Stir in the lime zest, lime juice, and green food coloring into the sugar mixture. Be cautious, as it may sizzle.
- Mix until well combined.

3. Shape the Lollipops:
- Line a baking sheet with parchment paper.
- Pour small rounds of the lime mixture onto the prepared sheet, leaving space for the leopard print decorations.
- Insert lollipop sticks into each round before the mixture completely hardens.

4. Create Leopard Print:
- Drizzle melted dark chocolate and white chocolate over the lime rounds to create a leopard print pattern. Use a toothpick to swirl the chocolates for a marbled effect.

5. Chill and Set:
- Allow the lollipops to cool and set at room temperature or expedite the process by placing them in the refrigerator for about 1-2 hours.

6. Serve:
- Once set, remove the lollipops from the parchment paper and serve. These make a delightful treat for Jumanji-themed parties or as a whimsical dessert for any occasion.

Nutrition Information:
Note: Nutritional values are approximate and may vary based on specific ingredients used.
- Serving Size: 1 lollipop
- Calories: 180
- Total Fat: 3g
- Saturated Fat: 2g
- Cholesterol: 0mg
- Sodium: 5mg
- Total Carbohydrates: 40g
- Dietary Fiber: 0g

- Sugars: 38g
- Protein: 0g

Indulge in the magic of Jumanji with these Leopard Lime Lollipops that promise a burst of citrusy goodness and a visually stunning leopard print that pays homage to the wild adventures of the jungle.

80. Baboon Basil Pesto

Embark on a culinary adventure inspired by the wild and whimsical world of Jumanji with our "Baboon Basil Pesto." Just like the unpredictable jungle in the film, this flavorful pesto brings together unexpected ingredients that create a delightful and adventurous twist on the classic basil pesto. Get ready to savor the taste of the untamed with this exotic and vibrant dish.

Serving: Ideal for 4 servings
Preparation Time: 15 minutes
Ready Time: 20 minutes

Ingredients:
- 2 cups fresh basil leaves, packed
- 1/2 cup roasted peanuts
- 1/3 cup Parmesan cheese, grated
- 1/3 cup sun-dried tomatoes, packed in oil, drained
- 2 cloves garlic, peeled
- 1/2 cup extra-virgin olive oil
- 1 tablespoon lemon juice
- Salt and pepper to taste
- 1/4 cup dried cranberries (optional, for a sweet twist)
- 1/4 cup grated coconut (optional, for added texture)

Instructions:
1. In a food processor, combine the fresh basil, roasted peanuts, Parmesan cheese, sun-dried tomatoes, and garlic. Pulse until the ingredients are finely chopped.
2. With the food processor running, slowly pour in the olive oil until the mixture becomes a smooth paste.

3. Add lemon juice, salt, and pepper to taste. Pulse a few more times to combine.
4. If you're feeling adventurous, add dried cranberries for a sweet and tangy kick, and grated coconut for an extra layer of texture. Pulse briefly to incorporate these optional ingredients.
5. Taste and adjust the seasoning if needed.
6. Transfer the Baboon Basil Pesto to a bowl, and it's ready to be served!

Nutrition Information:
Note: Nutrition information is approximate and may vary based on specific ingredients and optional add-ins.
- Calories: 250 per serving
- Fat: 22g
- Saturated Fat: 4g
- Cholesterol: 5mg
- Sodium: 150mg
- Carbohydrates: 8g
- Fiber: 2g
- Sugar: 3g
- Protein: 7g

Dive into the Jumanji-inspired world of Baboon Basil Pesto, where every bite is an adventure in flavor!

81. Elephant Ear Éclairs

Transport yourself into the adventurous world of Jumanji with these delightful Elephant Ear Éclairs. Inspired by the lush and exotic landscapes of the film, these éclairs are a sweet journey for your taste buds. With a crispy elephant ear pastry shell filled with a velvety vanilla cream, each bite is a cinematic experience. Enjoy the magic of Jumanji in every delicious mouthful!

Serving: Makes 12 Elephant Ear Éclairs
Preparation Time: 30 minutes
Ready Time: 2 hours

Ingredients:
For the Elephant Ear Pastry:

- 1 cup water
- 1/2 cup unsalted butter
- 1/4 teaspoon salt
- 1 cup all-purpose flour
- 4 large eggs

For the Vanilla Cream Filling:
- 2 cups whole milk
- 1/2 cup granulated sugar
- 1/4 cup cornstarch
- 1/4 teaspoon salt
- 4 large egg yolks
- 2 tablespoons unsalted butter
- 2 teaspoons vanilla extract

For the Glaze:
- 1 cup powdered sugar
- 2 tablespoons milk
- 1/2 teaspoon vanilla extract

Instructions:

Elephant Ear Pastry:
1. In a medium saucepan, combine water, butter, and salt. Bring to a boil over medium heat.
2. Add the flour all at once, stirring vigorously until the mixture forms a ball.
3. Remove from heat and let it cool for 5 minutes.
4. Add eggs, one at a time, beating well after each addition until smooth.
5. Preheat your oven to 400°F (200°C).
6. Pipe or spoon the pastry dough onto a baking sheet lined with parchment paper, forming 4-inch long strips.
7. Bake for 20-25 minutes or until golden brown and puffed. Allow to cool completely.

Vanilla Cream Filling:
1. In a saucepan, heat the milk until it's steaming but not boiling.
2. In a separate bowl, whisk together sugar, cornstarch, and salt. Add egg yolks and whisk until smooth.
3. Gradually pour the hot milk into the egg mixture, whisking constantly.
4. Return the mixture to the saucepan and cook over medium heat, whisking continuously until it thickens.
5. Remove from heat, stir in butter and vanilla extract. Let it cool completely.

Glaze:
1. In a small bowl, whisk together powdered sugar, milk, and vanilla extract until smooth.

Assembly:
1. Cut the cooled pastry shells in half horizontally.
2. Fill each shell with the vanilla cream filling using a piping bag or spoon.
3. Drizzle the glaze over the filled éclairs.
4. Allow the glaze to set for a few minutes before serving.

Nutrition Information:
(Per serving - 1 éclair)
- Calories: 280
- Total Fat: 16g
- Saturated Fat: 9g
- Cholesterol: 120mg
- Sodium: 150mg
- Total Carbohydrates: 28g
- Dietary Fiber: 0g
- Sugars: 18g
- Protein: 6g

Indulge in these Elephant Ear Éclairs as you embark on a culinary adventure inspired by the enchanting world of Jumanji!

82. Monkey Mocha Latte

Transport yourself into the adventurous world of Jumanji with this delightful Monkey Mocha Latte inspired by the mischievous monkeys in the film. This rich and indulgent beverage combines the bold flavors of chocolate and coffee, creating a drink that's as wild and exciting as the Jumanji jungle itself. Whether you're facing the challenges of the game or simply craving a delicious treat, the Monkey Mocha Latte is the perfect choice.

Serving: 2 servings
Preparation Time: 10 minutes
Ready Time: 15 minutes

Ingredients:
- 2 cups strong brewed coffee
- 1 cup whole milk
- 1/4 cup cocoa powder
- 1/4 cup sugar
- 1/2 cup whipped cream
- 1 teaspoon vanilla extract
- 1/2 cup chocolate chips
- 2 bananas, sliced
- Crushed ice
- Chocolate syrup (for garnish)

Instructions:
1. In a small saucepan, heat the milk over medium heat until it is warm but not boiling. Whisk in the cocoa powder and sugar until fully dissolved.
2. Add the chocolate chips to the warm milk mixture and stir continuously until the chocolate chips are melted and the mixture is smooth. Remove from heat and let it cool slightly.
3. Brew a strong cup of coffee. You can use an espresso machine or a French press to make a concentrated coffee.
4. In a blender, combine the brewed coffee, chocolate-milk mixture, vanilla extract, and a handful of ice. Blend until smooth and creamy.
5. Divide the sliced bananas between two glasses. Pour the Monkey Mocha Latte over the bananas.
6. Top each glass with a generous dollop of whipped cream and drizzle with chocolate syrup for an extra indulgent touch.
7. Serve immediately and enjoy the delightful blend of coffee, chocolate, and banana flavors inspired by the unpredictable world of Jumanji.

Nutrition Information (per serving):
- Calories: 280
- Total Fat: 12g
- Saturated Fat: 7g
- Trans Fat: 0g
- Cholesterol: 20mg
- Sodium: 60mg
- Total Carbohydrates: 40g
- Dietary Fiber: 4g
- Sugars: 25g

- Protein: 6g

Note: Nutrition information is approximate and may vary based on specific ingredients used.

83. Cobra Coconut Cupcakes

Step into the mystical world of Jumanji with these delightful Cobra Coconut Cupcakes. Inspired by the enchanting and adventurous atmosphere of the film, these cupcakes are a perfect blend of tropical flavors and a touch of danger, just like the game itself. Embark on a culinary journey as you indulge in these coconut-infused treats with a surprise cobra twist!

Serving: Makes 12 cupcakes
Preparation Time: 20 minutes
Ready Time: 40 minutes

Ingredients:
- 1 1/2 cups all-purpose flour
- 1 1/2 teaspoons baking powder
- 1/2 teaspoon baking soda
- 1/4 teaspoon salt
- 1 cup shredded coconut (sweetened)
- 1/2 cup unsalted butter, softened
- 1 cup granulated sugar
- 2 large eggs
- 1 teaspoon vanilla extract
- 1 cup coconut milk
- 12 cobra-shaped gummy candies (for decoration)

Instructions:
1. Preheat your oven to 350°F (175°C) and line a muffin tin with cupcake liners.
2. In a medium bowl, whisk together the flour, baking powder, baking soda, and salt. Stir in the shredded coconut.
3. In a separate large bowl, cream together the softened butter and sugar until light and fluffy.

4. Beat in the eggs, one at a time, and then add the vanilla extract. Mix until well combined.
5. Gradually add the dry ingredients to the wet ingredients, alternating with the coconut milk, beginning and ending with the dry ingredients. Mix until just combined.
6. Spoon the batter into the cupcake liners, filling each about two-thirds full.
7. Bake in the preheated oven for 18-20 minutes or until a toothpick inserted into the center comes out clean.
8. Allow the cupcakes to cool completely on a wire rack.

Decoration:
1. Once the cupcakes are cool, use a small knife to cut a small slit in the center of each cupcake.
2. Insert a cobra-shaped gummy candy into each slit, allowing it to peek out menacingly.

Nutrition Information:
(Per Serving)
- Calories: 280
- Total Fat: 15g
- Saturated Fat: 10g
- Trans Fat: 0g
- Cholesterol: 65mg
- Sodium: 220mg
- Total Carbohydrates: 34g
- Dietary Fiber: 1g
- Sugars: 20g
- Protein: 3g

Enjoy these Cobra Coconut Cupcakes as a sweet tribute to the Jumanji adventure, and let the flavors transport you to the heart of the jungle!

84. Quicksand Quiche Lorraine

Embark on a culinary adventure inspired by the enchanting world of Jumanji with our "Quicksand Quiche Lorraine." This savory delight pays homage to the unpredictable nature of the game, offering a taste experience that will transport you into the heart of the jungle. A rich blend of flavors awaits, capturing the essence of the iconic film and bringing it straight to your table.

Serving: 4-6 servings
Preparation Time: 15 minutes
Ready Time: 45 minutes

Ingredients:
- 1 pre-made pie crust (9 inches)
- 8 slices bacon, cooked and crumbled
- 1 cup shredded Swiss cheese
- 1/2 cup diced onion
- 1 tablespoon butter
- 1 1/2 cups half-and-half
- 4 large eggs
- 1/2 teaspoon salt
- 1/4 teaspoon black pepper
- 1/4 teaspoon ground nutmeg

Instructions:
1. Preheat your oven to 425°F (220°C).
2. In a medium-sized skillet, melt the butter over medium heat. Add diced onions and cook until they become translucent, about 3-4 minutes. Remove from heat and set aside.
3. Place the pre-made pie crust in a 9-inch pie dish, crimping the edges for a decorative touch.
4. In a mixing bowl, whisk together half-and-half, eggs, salt, black pepper, and ground nutmeg until well combined.
5. Spread the sautéed onions evenly over the bottom of the pie crust, followed by half of the crumbled bacon and half of the shredded Swiss cheese.
6. Pour the egg mixture over the layers of onions, bacon, and cheese.
7. Top with the remaining bacon and Swiss cheese, ensuring an even distribution.
8. Place the quiche in the preheated oven and bake for 15 minutes. Then, reduce the oven temperature to 350°F (175°C) and continue baking for an additional 25-30 minutes, or until the quiche is set and the top is golden brown.
9. Remove from the oven and let it cool for a few minutes before slicing.

Nutrition Information:
(Per serving)
- Calories: 380
- Total Fat: 28g
- Saturated Fat: 13g
- Trans Fat: 0g
- Cholesterol: 205mg
- Sodium: 630mg
- Total Carbohydrates: 17g
- Dietary Fiber: 1g
- Sugars: 2g
- Protein: 15g

Indulge in the Quicksand Quiche Lorraine as you immerse yourself in the magic of Jumanji, creating memories that blend the excitement of the film with the joy of a delicious homemade meal.

85. Tarzan Tofu Tacos

Step into the adventurous world of Jumanji with these Tarzan Tofu Tacos! Inspired by the lush and wild landscapes of the film, these tacos are a fusion of flavors that will transport you straight into the heart of the jungle. Packed with protein-rich tofu and vibrant, fresh ingredients, these tacos are a delightful journey for your taste buds.

Serving: Makes 4 servings
Preparation Time: 20 minutes
Ready Time: 35 minutes

Ingredients:
- 1 block extra-firm tofu, pressed and cubed
- 2 tablespoons soy sauce
- 1 tablespoon olive oil
- 1 teaspoon ground cumin
- 1 teaspoon smoked paprika
- 1 teaspoon garlic powder
- 1/2 teaspoon chili powder
- 1/2 teaspoon black pepper
- 1 tablespoon lime juice

- 8 small taco-sized flour tortillas
- 1 cup shredded lettuce
- 1 cup diced tomatoes
- 1 cup sliced bell peppers (assorted colors)
- 1/2 cup diced red onion
- 1/4 cup chopped fresh cilantro
- 1 avocado, sliced
- Lime wedges for garnish

Instructions:
1. In a bowl, combine cubed tofu, soy sauce, olive oil, cumin, smoked paprika, garlic powder, chili powder, black pepper, and lime juice. Toss until the tofu is well coated. Let it marinate for at least 10 minutes.
2. Heat a large skillet over medium-high heat. Add the marinated tofu and cook for 5-7 minutes, or until the tofu is golden brown and slightly crispy on the edges. Stir occasionally for even cooking.
3. Warm the flour tortillas in a dry skillet or microwave according to the package instructions.
4. Assemble the tacos by placing a spoonful of the cooked tofu on each tortilla. Top with shredded lettuce, diced tomatoes, sliced bell peppers, red onion, cilantro, and avocado.
5. Garnish with lime wedges for an extra burst of flavor.

Nutrition Information:
Note: Nutritional values are approximate and may vary based on specific ingredients used.
- Calories: 300 per serving
- Protein: 15g
- Fat: 12g
- Carbohydrates: 35g
- Fiber: 8g
- Sugar: 4g
- Sodium: 600mg

Embark on a culinary adventure with these Tarzan Tofu Tacos, bringing the spirit of Jumanji to your table. A perfect blend of textures and flavors that will leave you craving more!

86. Viper Veggie Volcano

Step into the wild and embark on a culinary adventure with the "Viper Veggie Volcano," inspired by the thrilling world of Jumanji. This explosive dish combines vibrant flavors and a medley of vegetables, creating a feast fit for jungle explorers. Get ready to tame the flavors of the wilderness and experience a taste journey that mirrors the excitement of the iconic Jumanji game.

Serving: 4 servings
Preparation Time: 20 minutes
Ready Time: 45 minutes

Ingredients:
- 1 large cauliflower, cut into florets
- 1 cup cherry tomatoes, halved
- 1 bell pepper, diced (any color)
- 1 zucchini, sliced
- 1 cup broccoli florets
- 1 cup snap peas, trimmed
- 2 tablespoons olive oil
- 1 teaspoon garlic powder
- 1 teaspoon onion powder
- 1 teaspoon smoked paprika
- Salt and pepper to taste
- 1 cup cooked quinoa or rice (optional, for serving)
- 1 cup shredded cheddar cheese (optional, for topping)
- Fresh cilantro or parsley, chopped (for garnish)

Instructions:
1. Preheat your oven to 400°F (200°C).
2. In a large mixing bowl, combine cauliflower florets, cherry tomatoes, diced bell pepper, zucchini slices, broccoli florets, and snap peas.
3. Drizzle the vegetables with olive oil and toss to coat evenly. Sprinkle garlic powder, onion powder, smoked paprika, salt, and pepper over the vegetables, tossing again to ensure even seasoning.
4. Spread the seasoned vegetables on a baking sheet in a single layer.
5. Roast in the preheated oven for 25-30 minutes or until the vegetables are tender and slightly caramelized, stirring halfway through.

6. If desired, serve the Viper Veggie Volcano over cooked quinoa or rice. Top with shredded cheddar cheese for an extra indulgent twist.
7. Garnish with fresh cilantro or parsley before serving.

Nutrition Information:
(Per serving without optional toppings)
- Calories: 180
- Total Fat: 8g
- Saturated Fat: 1.5g
- Trans Fat: 0g
- Cholesterol: 0mg
- Sodium: 60mg
- Total Carbohydrates: 24g
- Dietary Fiber: 7g
- Sugars: 6g
- Protein: 7g

Immerse yourself in the flavors of Jumanji with this Viper Veggie Volcano—a dish that captures the essence of the wild in every bite. It's a culinary escapade that will transport you to the heart of the jungle, making your dining experience an adventure of its own.

87. Leopard Lemon Lava Cake

Embark on a culinary adventure inspired by the thrilling world of Jumanji with our delectable Leopard Lemon Lava Cake. Just like the unpredictable twists and turns in the game, this dessert promises an explosion of flavors with a zesty lemony twist and a visually stunning leopard pattern. Whether you're a fan of the jungle or just a lover of all things sweet, this dessert is sure to transport you into a world of culinary magic.

Serving: Makes 4 servings
Preparation Time: 15 minutes
Ready Time: 30 minutes

Ingredients:
- 1 cup unsalted butter
- 8 oz white chocolate, chopped

- 1 cup granulated sugar
- 4 large eggs
- 1 teaspoon vanilla extract
- 1 cup all-purpose flour
- Zest of 2 lemons
- 2 tablespoons lemon juice
- 1/4 teaspoon salt
- Yellow and black food coloring (gel or liquid)

Instructions:
1. Preheat your oven to 350°F (175°C). Grease and flour four ramekins.
2. In a microwave-safe bowl, melt the butter and white chocolate together in 30-second intervals, stirring until smooth.
3. In a separate large bowl, whisk together the sugar, eggs, and vanilla extract until well combined.
4. Slowly pour the melted chocolate mixture into the egg mixture, stirring continuously.
5. Add the flour, lemon zest, lemon juice, and salt to the batter, and mix until just combined.
6. Divide the batter equally into two bowls. In one bowl, add yellow food coloring until you achieve a vibrant lemon yellow color. In the other bowl, add black food coloring until you achieve a deep, rich black color.
7. Spoon a layer of the yellow batter into each ramekin, followed by a dollop of the black batter in the center. Repeat this layering process until the ramekins are filled.
8. Use a toothpick or skewer to create a swirling pattern in the batter to resemble a leopard's spots.
9. Bake in the preheated oven for 20-25 minutes, or until the edges are set but the center is still slightly gooey.
10. Allow the cakes to cool for a few minutes before serving. Optionally, dust with powdered sugar or serve with a scoop of vanilla ice cream for an extra treat.

Nutrition Information:
(Per serving)
- Calories: 580
- Total Fat: 37g
- Saturated Fat: 22g
- Trans Fat: 0g
- Cholesterol: 180mg

- Sodium: 160mg
- Total Carbohydrates: 60g
- Dietary Fiber: 1g
- Sugars: 45g
- Protein: 7g

Indulge in this Leopard Lemon Lava Cake and let the magic of Jumanji unfold on your taste buds!

88. Water Buffalo Blue Cheese Burger

Step into the wild with the "Water Buffalo Blue Cheese Burger," inspired by the adventurous world of Jumanji. This mouthwatering burger combines the robust flavor of water buffalo meat with the bold kick of blue cheese, creating a savory experience that's as thrilling as a roll of the dice. Get ready to embark on a culinary journey that mirrors the excitement of the iconic board game.

Serving: 4 burgers
Preparation Time: 15 minutes
Ready Time: 30 minutes

Ingredients:
- 1 pound ground water buffalo meat
- 1/2 cup crumbled blue cheese
- 1/4 cup breadcrumbs
- 1/4 cup finely chopped red onion
- 2 cloves garlic, minced
- 1 tablespoon Worcestershire sauce
- 1 teaspoon Dijon mustard
- Salt and pepper to taste
- 4 burger buns
- Toppings: Lettuce, tomato slices, red onion rings

Instructions:
1. Preheat Grill or Stovetop Griddle:
- If using a grill, preheat to medium-high heat. If using a stovetop griddle, set it over medium-high heat.
2. Prepare the Burger Patties:

- In a large mixing bowl, combine the ground water buffalo meat, crumbled blue cheese, breadcrumbs, chopped red onion, minced garlic, Worcestershire sauce, Dijon mustard, salt, and pepper. Mix until well combined.

3. Form Patties:
- Divide the mixture into four equal portions and shape them into burger patties.

4. Cook the Patties:
- Cook the patties on the preheated grill or griddle for about 4-5 minutes per side or until they reach your desired level of doneness.

5. Toast the Burger Buns:
- In the last couple of minutes of cooking, place the burger buns on the grill or griddle to lightly toast.

6. Assemble the Burgers:
- Place each cooked patty on a toasted bun. Add lettuce, tomato slices, and red onion rings as desired.

7. Serve:
- Serve the Water Buffalo Blue Cheese Burgers hot, and enjoy the wild, savory flavors inspired by Jumanji.

Nutrition Information:
(Per serving)
- Calories: 450
- Protein: 25g
- Fat: 20g
- Carbohydrates: 40g
- Fiber: 3g
- Sugar: 5g
- Sodium: 800mg

Dive into the untamed flavors of Jumanji with this Water Buffalo Blue Cheese Burger, a culinary adventure that brings the spirit of the game to your plate.

89. Rhino Rainbow Rolls

Embark on a culinary adventure inspired by the wild and whimsical world of Jumanji with our Rhino Rainbow Rolls! These vibrant and flavorful rolls pay homage to the diverse landscapes and colorful characters encountered in the film. Packed with fresh ingredients, these rolls promise a taste journey that mirrors the excitement of the iconic game.

Serving: Makes approximately 4 servings.
Preparation Time: 30 minutes
Ready Time: 45 minutes

Ingredients:
For the Rainbow Rolls:
- 4 sheets of rice paper
- 1 cup cooked quinoa
- 1 large carrot, julienned
- 1 cucumber, julienned
- 1 red bell pepper, thinly sliced
- 1 avocado, sliced
- 1 cup purple cabbage, shredded
- 1 cup baby spinach leaves
- Fresh cilantro leaves (optional)
- Sesame seeds for garnish

For the Rhino Sauce:
- 3 tablespoons soy sauce
- 1 tablespoon sesame oil
- 1 tablespoon rice vinegar
- 1 tablespoon honey
- 1 teaspoon grated ginger
- 1 teaspoon minced garlic
- Pinch of red pepper flakes (optional)

Instructions:
1. Prepare the Rainbow Rolls:
a. Fill a shallow dish with warm water.
b. Dip one rice paper sheet into the water, ensuring it's fully submerged for about 10 seconds until it becomes pliable.
c. Carefully transfer the softened rice paper to a clean surface.
2. Layer the Ingredients:
a. Place a handful of quinoa in the center of the rice paper.
b. Arrange a small portion of each vegetable on top of the quinoa, creating a colorful line across the center.

c. Fold the sides of the rice paper over the filling and then roll it tightly from the bottom, creating a compact roll.
3. Repeat:
a. Repeat the process for the remaining rice paper sheets.
4. Prepare the Rhino Sauce:
a. In a small bowl, whisk together soy sauce, sesame oil, rice vinegar, honey, grated ginger, minced garlic, and red pepper flakes if desired.
5. Serve:
a. Cut the Rainbow Rolls in half diagonally and arrange them on a serving platter.
b. Drizzle the Rhino Sauce over the rolls and sprinkle with sesame seeds for garnish.

Nutrition Information:
(Per serving)
- Calories: 250
- Protein: 6g
- Carbohydrates: 40g
- Fiber: 6g
- Sugars: 8g
- Fat: 8g
- Saturated Fat: 1g
- Cholesterol: 0mg
- Sodium: 500mg

Embark on this culinary journey with Rhino Rainbow Rolls, a dish that captures the essence of Jumanji's vibrant and adventurous spirit. Enjoy the explosion of colors and flavors that mirror the magic of the game itself.

90. Python Peanut Butter Pie

Step into the wild and embark on a culinary adventure inspired by the fantastical world of Jumanji with our Python Peanut Butter Pie. This delectable dessert is a tribute to the exotic and unpredictable nature of the Jumanji jungle. Immerse yourself in the rich flavors and textures of this pie that will transport you to the heart of the game.

Serving: Serves 8

Preparation Time: 20 minutes
Ready Time: 4 hours (including chilling time)

Ingredients:
- 1 1/2 cups chocolate cookie crumbs
- 1/2 cup unsalted butter, melted
- 1 cup creamy peanut butter
- 1 package (8 oz) cream cheese, softened
- 1 cup powdered sugar
- 1 teaspoon vanilla extract
- 1 cup heavy cream
- 1 cup semi-sweet chocolate chips
- Python-inspired chocolate decor (optional)

Instructions:
1. Prepare the Crust:
- In a medium bowl, combine the chocolate cookie crumbs and melted butter.
- Press the mixture into the bottom of a pie dish to form a crust. Chill in the refrigerator while preparing the filling.
2. Make the Filling:
- In a large mixing bowl, beat together the peanut butter, cream cheese, powdered sugar, and vanilla extract until smooth and well combined.
3. Whip the Cream:
- In a separate bowl, whip the heavy cream until stiff peaks form.
4. Combine Fillings:
- Gently fold the whipped cream into the peanut butter mixture until fully incorporated.
5. Add Chocolate Chips:
- Fold in the semi-sweet chocolate chips to add a delightful crunch and extra layer of flavor.
6. Assemble the Pie:
- Pour the peanut butter filling into the chilled crust, spreading it evenly.
7. Chill:
- Place the pie in the refrigerator and let it chill for at least 4 hours or until set.
8. Decorate (Optional):
- For an extra touch, decorate the top of the pie with Python-inspired chocolate decor.
9. Serve:

- Once fully chilled and set, slice and serve the Python Peanut Butter Pie to your fellow adventurers.

Nutrition Information:
(Per Serving)
- Calories: 480
- Total Fat: 38g
- Saturated Fat: 18g
- Trans Fat: 0g
- Cholesterol: 60mg
- Sodium: 220mg
- Total Carbohydrates: 28g
- Dietary Fiber: 3g
- Sugars: 18g
- Protein: 10g

Embark on this culinary journey inspired by Jumanji, and let the Python Peanut Butter Pie tantalize your taste buds with every adventurous bite!

91. Baboon Black Bean Brownies

Transport yourself into the heart of the jungle with these delectable Baboon Black Bean Brownies, inspired by the wild and whimsical world of Jumanji. Packed with the goodness of black beans, these brownies are a treat for the taste buds and a nod to the adventures that unfold within the game. Perfect for movie nights or themed parties, these brownies are sure to be a hit among Jumanji enthusiasts and dessert lovers alike.

Serving: Makes 12 brownies
Preparation Time: 15 minutes
Ready Time: 45 minutes

Ingredients:
- 1 can (15 ounces) black beans, drained and rinsed
- 3 large eggs
- 1/3 cup melted coconut oil
- 1/4 cup cocoa powder
- 1/8 teaspoon salt
- 2 teaspoons vanilla extract

- 1/2 cup granulated sugar
- 1/2 cup chocolate chips
- 1/3 cup chopped walnuts (optional)
- Cooking spray for greasing the pan

Instructions:
1. Preheat your oven to 350°F (175°C). Grease an 8x8-inch baking pan with cooking spray.
2. In a food processor, combine the black beans, eggs, melted coconut oil, cocoa powder, salt, and vanilla extract. Blend until smooth and well combined.
3. Add the granulated sugar to the mixture and blend again until the batter is creamy.
4. Fold in the chocolate chips and chopped walnuts (if using) into the batter, ensuring an even distribution.
5. Pour the batter into the prepared baking pan, spreading it evenly.
6. Bake in the preheated oven for 30-35 minutes or until a toothpick inserted into the center comes out with moist crumbs, but not wet batter.
7. Allow the brownies to cool in the pan for about 10 minutes before transferring them to a wire rack to cool completely.
8. Once cooled, cut into 12 squares and serve.

Nutrition Information:
Per Serving (1 brownie):
- Calories: 180
- Total Fat: 9g
- Saturated Fat: 6g
- Cholesterol: 47mg
- Sodium: 67mg
- Total Carbohydrates: 22g
- Dietary Fiber: 3g
- Sugars: 12g
- Protein: 4g

Note: Nutrition information is approximate and may vary based on specific ingredients used.

92. Elephant Eye Edamame

Step into the magical world of Jumanji with the delightful and whimsical "Elephant Eye Edamame." Inspired by the enchanting film, this dish brings a touch of adventure to your dining table. Just like the unpredictable game itself, these Elephant Eye Edamame are a surprising and delicious treat that will transport you to the heart of the jungle with every bite.

Serving: 4 servings
Preparation Time: 15 minutes
Ready Time: 20 minutes

Ingredients:
- 2 cups edamame pods, fresh or frozen
- 2 tablespoons olive oil
- 1 teaspoon sesame oil
- 2 cloves garlic, minced
- 1 tablespoon soy sauce
- 1 teaspoon honey
- 1/2 teaspoon ginger, grated
- 1/2 teaspoon chili flakes (adjust to taste)
- Salt, to taste
- Black sesame seeds, for garnish
- Chopped green onions, for garnish

Instructions:
1. Prepare the Edamame:
If using fresh edamame, boil them in salted water for about 5-7 minutes until tender. If using frozen edamame, follow the package instructions to cook. Drain and set aside.
2. Sauté the Aromatics:
In a large skillet, heat olive oil and sesame oil over medium heat. Add minced garlic and grated ginger, sautéing until fragrant.
3. Add Edamame:
Toss in the cooked edamame, ensuring they are well coated with the garlic and ginger-infused oil.
4. Season the Edamame:
Drizzle soy sauce and honey over the edamame. Sprinkle chili flakes and salt to taste. Stir well to combine, allowing the flavors to meld for a few minutes.
5. Garnish:

Once the edamame are coated and heated through, transfer them to a serving dish. Garnish with black sesame seeds and chopped green onions for a burst of color and added flavor.

6. Serve:

Your Elephant Eye Edamame is ready to serve! Enjoy this unique and flavorful dish as a snack, appetizer, or side dish.

Nutrition Information:

Note: Nutritional values are approximate and may vary based on specific ingredients and preparation methods.

- Calories per serving: 180
- Total Fat: 12g
- Saturated Fat: 1.5g
- Trans Fat: 0g
- Cholesterol: 0mg
- Sodium: 400mg
- Total Carbohydrates: 12g
- Dietary Fiber: 6g
- Sugars: 3g
- Protein: 8g

Embrace the spirit of Jumanji with this Elephant Eye Edamame dish, a delightful nod to the wonders of the jungle. Whether you're hosting a movie night or simply seeking a unique and flavorful snack, this recipe is sure to please both kids and adults alike.

93. Monkey Maple Syrup

Embark on a culinary adventure inspired by the wild and enchanting world of Jumanji with our delightful "Monkey Maple Syrup." Just like the unpredictable and lively nature of the game, this unique syrup is a playful twist on the classic maple flavor, bringing a touch of the jungle to your breakfast table. Infused with the spirit of Jumanji, this recipe promises a tantalizing experience that will transport you to the heart of the mysterious board game.

Serving: Makes approximately 1 cup of Monkey Maple Syrup.
Preparation Time: 15 minutes
Ready Time: 20 minutes

Ingredients:
- 1 cup pure maple syrup
- 1 ripe banana, mashed
- 1/2 cup chopped walnuts
- 1/4 cup coconut flakes
- 1 tablespoon butter
- 1 teaspoon vanilla extract
- 1/2 teaspoon ground cinnamon
- Pinch of salt

Instructions:
1. In a saucepan over medium heat, melt the butter.
2. Add the mashed banana and cook for 2-3 minutes until it becomes fragrant and slightly caramelized.
3. Pour in the maple syrup, stirring well to combine with the banana.
4. Add the chopped walnuts, coconut flakes, vanilla extract, ground cinnamon, and a pinch of salt. Continue to stir, ensuring all ingredients are evenly distributed.
5. Allow the mixture to simmer for 10-12 minutes, or until it thickens to your desired consistency.
6. Remove from heat and let it cool slightly.
7. Strain the syrup to remove any banana fibers, leaving you with a smooth Monkey Maple Syrup.
8. Transfer the syrup to a jar or serving container.

Nutrition Information:
Note: Nutrition values are approximate and may vary based on specific ingredients used.
- Serving Size: 2 tablespoons
- Calories: 120
- Total Fat: 6g
- Saturated Fat: 2g
- Cholesterol: 5mg
- Sodium: 30mg
- Total Carbohydrates: 17g
- Dietary Fiber: 1g
- Sugars: 14g
- Protein: 1g

Indulge in the wild flavors of Jumanji with this Monkey Maple Syrup, a delectable concoction that captures the essence of the jungle in every drop. Perfect for drizzling over pancakes, waffles, or even as a unique topping for desserts. Get ready to roll the dice and savor the magic of Jumanji at your breakfast table!

94. Jungle Jicama Salad

Embark on a culinary adventure inspired by the untamed beauty of the Jumanji jungle with this vibrant and refreshing Jungle Jicama Salad. Just like the unpredictable twists and turns in the iconic film, this salad offers a delightful blend of textures and flavors, transporting you to a world of exotic tastes.

Serving: 4 servings
Preparation Time: 20 minutes
Ready Time: 25 minutes

Ingredients:
- 1 medium jicama, peeled and julienned
- 1 cup pineapple chunks
- 1 cup cherry tomatoes, halved
- 1 cucumber, thinly sliced
- 1/2 red onion, thinly sliced
- 1/2 cup cilantro leaves, chopped
- 1/4 cup mint leaves, chopped
- 1/2 cup roasted peanuts, chopped
- 1 avocado, diced

Dressing:
- 3 tablespoons olive oil
- 2 tablespoons lime juice
- 1 tablespoon honey
- 1 teaspoon grated ginger
- Salt and pepper to taste

Instructions:
1. In a large bowl, combine the jicama, pineapple chunks, cherry tomatoes, cucumber, red onion, cilantro, mint, and roasted peanuts.

2. In a separate small bowl, whisk together the olive oil, lime juice, honey, grated ginger, salt, and pepper to create the dressing.
3. Pour the dressing over the salad and toss gently to coat the ingredients evenly.
4. Carefully fold in the diced avocado to avoid mushing.
5. Allow the flavors to meld for about 5 minutes before serving.
6. Serve the Jungle Jicama Salad in individual bowls, garnished with extra cilantro and mint leaves if desired.

Nutrition Information:
(Per serving)
- Calories: 250
- Protein: 5g
- Fat: 15g
- Carbohydrates: 28g
- Fiber: 9g
- Sugar: 10g
- Vitamin C: 45mg
- Iron: 2mg

Indulge in the wild side of flavor with this Jungle Jicama Salad, a dish that mirrors the excitement and unpredictability of the Jumanji universe. Bursting with freshness and nutritional goodness, this salad is the perfect addition to your repertoire of adventurous recipes.

95. Cobra Cornbread

Transport your taste buds to the heart of the Jumanji jungle with our exotic and adventurous Cobra Cornbread! Inspired by the wild and mysterious world of Jumanji, this cornbread is infused with bold flavors and a touch of daring spice. The name pays homage to the elusive cobra that lurks in the depths of the jungle, embodying the thrill of the game itself. Get ready for a culinary adventure that mirrors the excitement of Jumanji!

Serving: - Serves: 8-10
Preparation Time: - 15 minutes
Ready Time: - 40 minutes

Ingredients:
- 2 cups cornmeal
- 1 cup all-purpose flour
- 1 tablespoon baking powder
- 1 teaspoon baking soda
- 1 teaspoon salt
- 1/2 cup unsalted butter, melted
- 1/4 cup honey
- 1 1/2 cups buttermilk
- 2 large eggs
- 1 cup corn kernels (fresh or frozen)
- 1/2 cup diced jalapeños
- 1/2 cup shredded sharp cheddar cheese
- 1/4 cup chopped fresh cilantro

Instructions:
1. Preheat your oven to 375°F (190°C). Grease a 9x13 inch baking dish.
2. In a large mixing bowl, combine the cornmeal, all-purpose flour, baking powder, baking soda, and salt.
3. In a separate bowl, whisk together the melted butter, honey, buttermilk, and eggs.
4. Pour the wet ingredients into the dry ingredients and stir until just combined.
5. Fold in the corn kernels, diced jalapeños, shredded cheddar cheese, and chopped cilantro.
6. Pour the batter into the prepared baking dish, spreading it evenly.
7. Bake in the preheated oven for 25-30 minutes or until a toothpick inserted into the center comes out clean.
8. Allow the Cobra Cornbread to cool for 10 minutes before slicing and serving.

Nutrition Information:
- Calories per serving: 320
- Total Fat: 15g
- Saturated Fat: 8g
- Cholesterol: 70mg
- Sodium: 600mg
- Total Carbohydrates: 40g
- Dietary Fiber: 3g
- Sugars: 9g

- Protein: 8g

Embrace the spirit of Jumanji with this Cobra Cornbread that captures the essence of adventure in every delicious bite!

96. Vulture Vanilla Vinaigrette

Embark on a culinary adventure inspired by the wild and whimsical world of Jumanji with our "Vulture Vanilla Vinaigrette." This exotic dressing pays homage to the film's mysterious and enchanting atmosphere, combining unexpected flavors to transport your taste buds on a journey of their own.

Serving: Ideal for salads, drizzle this vinaigrette over mixed greens or use it as a marinade for grilled chicken or vegetables. The possibilities are as limitless as the adventures in the jungle.
Preparation Time: 15 minutes
Ready Time: 15 minutes

Ingredients:
- 1/2 cup extra-virgin olive oil
- 1/4 cup balsamic vinegar
- 1 tablespoon honey
- 1 teaspoon Dijon mustard
- 1/2 teaspoon vanilla extract
- 1/4 teaspoon ground cinnamon
- 1/8 teaspoon ground black pepper
- Pinch of salt
- 1 small garlic clove, minced
- Zest of one orange
- Optional: 1 tablespoon finely chopped fresh herbs (such as basil or thyme)

Instructions:
1. In a bowl, whisk together the olive oil, balsamic vinegar, honey, Dijon mustard, and vanilla extract until well combined.
2. Add the ground cinnamon, black pepper, and a pinch of salt, whisking again to incorporate the dry ingredients.

3. Stir in the minced garlic and orange zest, combining the flavors for a delightful twist.
4. For an extra layer of freshness, add finely chopped fresh herbs of your choice, such as basil or thyme.
5. Taste the vinaigrette and adjust the seasoning as needed. If you prefer a sweeter flavor, add more honey; for a tangier kick, increase the Dijon mustard.
6. Once satisfied with the taste, transfer the vinaigrette to a bottle or jar with a tight-fitting lid.
7. Allow the vinaigrette to chill in the refrigerator for at least 15 minutes to let the flavors meld.
8. Shake well before serving and drizzle over your favorite salad or use as a marinade for grilled dishes.

Nutrition Information:
(Per 2-tablespoon serving)
- Calories: 120
- Fat: 11g
- Saturated Fat: 1.5g
- Cholesterol: 0mg
- Sodium: 50mg
- Carbohydrates: 5g
- Fiber: 0g
- Sugars: 4g
- Protein: 0g

Enjoy the magic of Jumanji with each delightful bite of this Vulture Vanilla Vinaigrette, bringing a touch of the jungle to your table.

CONCLUSION

In conclusion, the culinary journey through "Jumanji Feast: 96 Culinary Marvels Inspired by the Film" has been nothing short of a fantastical adventure for both the kitchen enthusiast and the film aficionado. The marriage of cinematic wonder and gastronomic creativity has birthed a collection of 96 food ideas that not only pay homage to the iconic Jumanji franchise but also transcend the boundaries of ordinary cookbooks.

One cannot help but marvel at the ingenious ways in which the author has translated the enchanting world of Jumanji into a tangible and delectable experience. Each recipe is a culinary masterpiece, carefully crafted to capture the essence of the film and transport the reader into the heart of the jungle. From the savory delights inspired by the lush landscapes to the sweet indulgences that mirror the whimsical creatures of Jumanji, this cookbook is a testament to the author's dedication to creating an immersive and delightful gastronomic adventure.

The cookbook goes beyond mere recipes; it is a celebration of the magic of storytelling through both film and food. The clever incorporation of Jumanji's diverse characters, landscapes, and mystical elements into the culinary creations adds a layer of depth and excitement that sets this cookbook apart. Whether you are a seasoned chef or a novice in the kitchen, the clear and detailed instructions make it accessible to cooks of all skill levels, inviting them to embark on their own culinary escapade.

Moreover, "Jumanji Feast" does not just focus on the final product but also emphasizes the joy of the cooking process. The anecdotes and trivia sprinkled throughout the book provide delightful insights into the making of the film, creating a connection between the recipes and the cinematic universe. It's more than a cookbook; it's a journey of discovery, a narrative woven through the art of cooking, inviting readers to explore the realms of taste and imagination.

The versatility of the recipes ensures that there is something for everyone, catering to a wide range of tastes and dietary preferences. The cookbook effortlessly combines comfort food with exotic flavors, making it a treasure trove for those seeking culinary diversity. Each page beckons with the promise of a new, exciting dish waiting to be savored, making "Jumanji Feast" a timeless addition to any kitchen library.

As we close the pages of this extraordinary cookbook, the lingering taste of adventure and the aroma of exotic spices stay with us. "Jumanji Feast" not only offers a delightful array of recipes but also serves as a reminder of the magic that happens when creativity knows no bounds. It invites us to break free from the ordinary and embrace the extraordinary, both in the kitchen and in our daily lives.

In the end, "Jumanji Feast: 96 Culinary Marvels Inspired by the Film" is more than a cookbook—it's a celebration of imagination, a feast for the senses, and a tribute to the enduring appeal of Jumanji. As we bid farewell to the culinary journey within its pages, we are left inspired to bring a touch of enchantment and adventure to our own kitchens, turning every meal into a celebration of the extraordinary.

Milton Keynes UK
Ingram Content Group UK Ltd.
UKHW010028090224
437518UK00012B/1000